Praise for *Master*

"*Master Your Code stretches beyond th ...p book. Darren works from a fundame ... Great leaders must master themselves before they can effectively lead others. He brings that thesis to life in a powerful way.* This is a book I'd recommend to anyone interested in learning about leadership and human potential."
— Frank Blake, Former Chairman & CEO, The Home Depot

"*I've experienced Darren unleashing the power of a team by helping the individual members put unproductive beliefs and behaviors aside. I can't make a better world unless I can be a better me. **Master Your Code is a deeply insightful yet completely practical guide to that better self.*** Do you owe that to the people around you? This is a very special book!*"
— Bill Anderson, CEO, Roche Pharmaceuticals

"*Warning: object in mirror (that's you) may be closer than it appears...to not reaching (your) full potential! **Those who want to change this outcome need to read this book!***"
— Calvin McDonald, CEO, Lululemon

"*All of us have layers of hidden biological, cultural, and emotional programming. Left unexamined, this programming drives our behavior and limits our potential. But it doesn't have to do so. **Master Your Code draws on wisdom new and old, offering a practical guide for exploring your own 'code'** and – as Darren compellingly demonstrates from his own experience – how to take control and rewrite it for the life you want to lead.*"
— Drew Houston, CEO, Dropbox

"*This book makes a very bold promise – everyone has the potential to lead an extraordinary life. And **Darren delivers in a way that few books do.** Master Your Code does what it suggests. It combines ancient wisdom and modern science to deliver an essential guidebook for what we all want – a life of joy, fulfillment, and happiness.*"
— Sukhinder Singh Cassidy, President, StubHub

"*Master Your Code is the most important thing I've read in years. **Some books show you the ceiling and how to break through it. This books shows that there is no ceiling.***"
— Tim Chen, CEO, NerdWallet

"*Too many of us plateau in our progress, falling short of what we once hoped for.* **This book can help your life be the rocket ship it was supposed to be.** *Read it to operate at your highest point of contribution.*"

— Greg McKeown, author of Essentialism

"**If you want to be a better leader, a better person – and you're not sure what is holding you back – this book is the unlock you are looking for.** *Master Your Code has powerful examples to learn from, written from the heart of Darren's personal journey. If you're willing to listen, learn, reflect and commit,* **you have the ability to go from average to extraordinary.**"

— Heidi Zak, Co-Founder & CEO, ThirdLove

"*I couldn't put this book down. Truly authentic, important, and inspiring, Master Your Code is not just another leadership tome – it is a timely "code breaker." Darren invites readers into his personal life as the humanistic underpinning to the genius guidance he delivers.* **Dive in with an open mind and be transported into a new world that offers provocative insights and shares a practical guide for you to unlock your own code, and guide those around you to unlock theirs.**"

— G. Kelly O'Dea, Chairman Emeritus,
Outward Bound International

"**Darren challenges us to fundamentally change the way we look at the decisions we make and the lives we lead.** *His honest, raw testimony and personal revelations required courage that few people possess.* **Whether you are young or old, struggling or successful, this is a book you will treasure.**"

— Thomas Friel, Former Chairman & CEO, Heidrick & Struggles

"*Darren's* **personal insights and bold present relevance have helped transform me as a person and leader.** *This book captures the essence of his insights into personal development and the power of agency and choice. We can choose to rewrite our code and change our trajectory now!*"

— Scott Cutler, CEO, StockX

"*Master Your Code is truly transformational. It's the kind of book that opens up unlimited possibilities for who you can be, creates a major shift in how you think about your potential, and helps orchestrate your moves toward realizing an extraordinary life.* **I consider it one of the great personal development books of our generation, and one that will become timeless.**"

— *Amy Buckner Chowdry, CEO, AnswerLab*

"*Darren presents a straightforward, but immensely sophisticated guide to becoming the best version of yourself. This book is presented in a step-by-step format, framing a set of principles, which are grounded in data and reference. It was relevant the moment I finished the first chapter, and rich enough to be a guide for years to come. It has* **transformed how I lead and partner, both in the the office and at home.** *It's a remarkable tool.*"

— *Perkins Miller, CEO, Fandom*

"**Darren's inspiring story didn't happen by accident. His dedication to mastering his code and changing his life, and the lives of those around him, is incredible.** *As an entrepreneur I've had to recalculate and rework my own internal coding and that of my business many times to reach the next level of success. Master Your Code provides great insight on exactly how to go about that extremely important process.*"

— *Nina Vaca, Chairman & CEO, Pinnacle Group*

"*I have experienced first-hand the results of these accessible teachings. The breakthrough is empowering. What has held me back were my own false beliefs that I held as truth. Just realizing that alone has unlocked exciting opportunities that make me jump out of bed every morning.* **My only regret is that this book wasn't written sooner.**"

— *Ben Goorin, President, Goorin Bros.*

"*This is a provocative and empowering work. Drawing on a compelling balance of science, intuition, and intense personal experience, Darren challenges us to examine the programming that drives our behavior...and ultimately our lives.* **This book will likely cause some uncomfortable introspection, but is well worth the effort. There is something for everyone here.**"

— *Jeff Cohen, CEO, Larson-Juhl*
(a Berkshire Hathaway company)

"Allergic to self-help books that evangelize stale maxims? Fatigued by blogs, articles and podcasts that are impossible to keep up with, or distinguish as truly valuable? If so, read this book! **Master Your Code is a refreshingly crisp and approachable guide to a fundamental reframing of life's most obstinate patterns.** The book thoughtfully weaves in Darren's incredible personal experience and the best of classical teachings, leaving the reader inspired and energized."

— *Seth Cohen, President & Co-Founder, OODA Health*

"Despite success in most areas of life, I've quickly realized after reading Master Your Code that I'm operating at half my potential. This book has helped me see how my own thoughts are getting in the way. **I've never been so invigorated by a single book and so inspired to start new patterns for my future. Master Your Code is going to be added to the three books that everyone in my company reads.**"

— *Mike Faith, CEO, Headsets.com*

"**Master Your Code is a book for everyone**, but especially for those who might not be drawn to more typical self-help style books. Using powerful real-life examples, Darren shows "the why" in a refreshingly approachable way and provides readers a toolkit to reframe their thinking to achieve their fullest potential."

— *Christina Stembel, founder & CEO, Farmgirl Flowers*

Master Your Code

Master Your Code

THE ART, WISDOM, AND SCIENCE
OF LEADING AN EXTRAORDINARY LIFE

Darren J. Gold

Printed by B.C. Allen Publishing and Tonic Books
144 N 7th St. #525
Brooklyn, NY 11249

Now taking manuscript submissions and book ideas at any stage of the process:

submissions@tonicbooks.online

Printed in the United States of America

Cover Design: Vanessa Maynard
Interior Design: Susan Veach

ISBN: 978-1-950977-92-5

Contents

Master Your Code

program
/ˈprōˌgram/
noun

A set of subconscious, safety-based beliefs, values, and rules that automatically drive your behavior and limit your results

code
/kōd/
noun

A consciously chosen set of beliefs, values, and rules that is purposefully designed to serve you and produce extraordinary results

extraordinary
/ik-ˈstrȯr-də-ˌner-ē, ek-strə-ˈȯr- də-ˌner-ē /
adjective

Very unusual or remarkable

Synonyms: Exceptional, amazing, astonishing, astounding, marvelous, wonderful, sensational, stunning, incredible, unbelievable, miraculous, phenomenal, prodigious, spectacular

Introduction

No man is free who is not master of himself.
—Epictetus

I am blessed to lead an extraordinary life. This hasn't always been the case. I grew up on the edge of poverty in a highly dysfunctional family. I was a child of divorced, uneducated parents who periodically spent time in jail. I lived in three different countries and more than a dozen homes before the age of twelve. Growing up, I was surrounded by crime, addiction, and financial insecurity.

Today, I am sought out by the CEOs of many of the world's leading companies to help them take their performance in all aspects of their lives to the next level. More importantly, I have been married to a wonderful woman for the last twenty-four years, and together we have raised three healthy, thriving children. My work, my personal life, and my purpose are all completely aligned. And I feel like my journey has only just begun.

How does this happen? How does anyone get to a point where he can say unequivocally that he feels fulfilled and fully alive? Why are some leaders more effective than others? Why are certain individuals more prone to depression while others seem to possess a magical resilience? Why do some elite athletes become professionals and others remain amateurs? Why are some of us happy—in our relationships, careers, and lives—and others unhappy despite almost identical circumstances?

I have spent the past decade deeply examining these questions, and *Master Your Code* is my attempt at providing the answers. It will take reading the whole book to fully appreciate what I've discovered about the art and science of leading an extraordinary life, but let me offer a quick preview of what's to come.

Every single person is run by a subconscious program of her own making. Even your doubts right now about the promise of this book are part of your program (I'll explain that in a bit). The only difference between the average person and the person who is leading an extraordinary life is the following: *The average person is run by her program and doesn't even know it. The extraordinary person rewrites her program and becomes the master of her code.* That's it. It's that simple, and that difficult.

Think back to the year of your birth. You didn't know it at the time, but from the moment you were born, you began to accumulate a set of beliefs, values, and rules designed to help you make sense of the crazy world you had just entered. Each day, you accumulated new rules, which you stacked on top of the old ones. Decades later, you have literally thousands of rules that together determine how you make meaning of your environment, how you behave, and what results you get. Think of this stack of rules as the computer program that runs your life.

There are three essential things you need to know about your program:

1. Every single part of your program was subconsciously constructed in response to your environment.

2. Almost all of your program is designed to avoid risk and keep you safe. This makes sense; it's how the human species has survived.

3. Since your program is entirely made up, you have the ability to rewrite or reconstruct any part of it. Very few people realize this. And even fewer know how to go about doing it.

This book will show you how to rewrite your program. In my experience as a CEO and now as an advisor to leaders of some of the world's best-known organizations, I have found that of the thousands of beliefs, values, and rules that control you, there are ten that matter most. This book will show you what the ten are and how to rewrite them. You will discover that doing so gives you the freedom and power to control and shape your life. Rather than being driven by an outdated program, you will be the master of your code. This will transform your relationships, your career, your overall well-being. You will see yourself, others, and your environment in a completely different way. A whole new world of possibilities will open up.

Mastering your code changes everything. I have seen it transform a challenging life into one of unlimited potential, a relatively good life into one that is truly extraordinary. It can turn an uninterested student into an avid learner. It can resurrect a lifeless relationship, making it passionate and joyful. And it can transform a manager into a leader.

***

I grew up with a father who at age fourteen dropped out of school and turned to a life of crime. For a number of years, my father and I shared a one-bedroom apartment in a tough area of the San Fernando Valley in Los Angeles. When I turned thirteen, my dad gave me a birthday present—a loaded shotgun that he insisted I keep by my bed, just in case someone tried to break in while we were sleeping.

{My Rule: The world is
a dangerous place}[1]

When the phone rang, as it often did, my job was to lie to the bill collectors so they would stop calling. The lie that worked best was that my dad had just passed away and that any attempt to collect money would be a waste of time. In addition to avoiding bill collectors, my father's specialty was counterfeiting. One of the many ways he used this skill was to create fake insurance cards. This was the era before electronic billing systems, so we would switch from one doctor's office to the next to receive health care, never paying a dime. My dad found a way, however unconventional, to make sure I felt cared for and safe.

{My Rule: Do whatever it takes to
protect your family}

Notwithstanding (or perhaps because of) this upbringing, I somehow became an exceptional student at school. I was determined to grow up and have a different life.

{My Rule: There is nothing more
important than education}

And I managed to do it. I was student body president

---

1   Throughout the book, {My Rule} will be used to designate a line of programming specific to me and {Rule} will refer to the programming of the reader more generally. {Rule} will be used to note where a specific line of a program is being examined and rewritten.

of my large public L.A. high school. I was the first in my family to go to college. I attended law school. I spent time at the famous consulting firm McKinsey & Company and then became a partner at a prestigious private equity firm. By my midthirties, I was serving on several company boards, was responsible for investing and managing hundreds of millions of dollars of capital, and was earning more money than I ever thought possible. I had made it. I had it all. A wonderful wife, three healthy children, professional success, and financial security. I was at the top of my game. Or so I thought.

One day, I walked into my CEO's office and was summarily fired for no real reason. I have my theories, but it doesn't matter. At that point, my life as I knew it was shattered. A big part of my identity had been wrapped up in my professional success.

{My Rule: Do whatever it takes to be successful and financially secure}

Now that was gone. This was the first real failure of my life, and it was a big one. For the first time in my career, I began truly to doubt myself. I lost my confidence, my edge. The business environment at the time didn't help the situation; the economy had just entered the worst recession since the Great Depression.

The good news is that I finally had time for some much-needed reflection. I began to realize that I had a choice about how to make meaning from my firing, a choice that would have massive ramifications in my life. I could choose the easy path of blame, resentment, anger, and frustration. Or I could take a hard look inward, at my own responsibility for my life and how it was unfolding. I chose the latter.

Over the next several months, it became increasingly clear that I had been living a life—a good one, no doubt—that I hadn't consciously chosen. I was running on autopilot, with some underlying program driving me. And while this program had kept me safe and served me well, it had reached the limits of its effectiveness. There was much more that I could give, become, and experience in every part of my life. I realized then that I could update my program, that I could choose to see myself and my situation in any way I wanted. I didn't have to live according to a set of rules written by a seven-year-old boy—a program designed to protect me from the intense uncertainty and unpredictability of a dysfunctional and unorthodox upbringing. Instead, I could be the master of a code that would produce extraordinary results in my life.

That realization took a few years to fully unfold, but it changed everything for me. Without it, I likely would have continued to hunker down, choosing a path that kept me safe and minimized risk. I would have chosen to play small. To play not to lose, rather than playing to win. Instead I began to see, for the first time, that I had deeply held beliefs and rules about myself and how the world worked. I began to understand where those rules came from. I saw how they had served me and where they limited me. And, most importantly, I discovered that I could modify them. I realized that there was no innate truth to any part of my program. The question wasn't whether my beliefs and rules were true, but rather whether they served me. I had been asking the wrong question all along.

My discovery that I was run by a program and that I could rewrite it transformed who I am. Today, my work is totally aligned with my purpose—impacting the lives of others by unlocking their full potential. I have deepened the relationships with the people I care about most. And I am living life more fully than ever before.

I have spent the past decade devoted to mastering my code, and I am by no means done. Yet this commitment to self-mastery has completely altered who I am as a leader, a parent, a husband, a son, a brother, a friend, and a colleague. *Master Your Code* is the product of that commitment. The impact of rewriting my program has been so profound that it has become my mission to share it with the world—professionally and personally.

The most fundamental choice you can make in your life is to master your code. To consciously choose the beliefs, values, and rules that determine the results you will get. No matter what the conditions of your current life are—you may be really struggling or insanely successful—the odds are that your life isn't optimized because you are run by a program you've assembled subconsciously. Think about it this way: You undoubtedly have a conscious vision, vague or extremely clear, of the life you want to live. Most likely, however, you are subconsciously being driven by a program that has a low probability of producing that vision.

Perhaps you want to become a leader in your company, or pursue your dream to become an artist, or reignite the passion with your spouse. I guarantee you this: No matter how committed you are to your vision, the odds of it happening on its own are low. If you truly want to lead an extraordinary life, you must explore your program and consciously choose your code. The actions available to you will expand massively. The greater the range of actions, the greater the probability you'll achieve the results you want.

I wrote this book for those of you who want to lead

a fulfilling and effective life, and who are willing to take on the responsibility of authoring it. I did not write it for the timid or faint of heart, or for those who think they have it all figured out. Rather, it's for those of you with the maturity, humility, and courage to question even your most deeply held parts. You know who you are. The world needs more of you.

How to Read This Book

Master Your Code is divided into ten chapters. Each will explore how a single line of your program drives and limits your effectiveness. It will then invite you to make a choice to rewrite and replace lines that are no longer working for you. The result will be a code—your code—for leading an extraordinary life.

The average person who is run by a program believes ...	The extraordinary person who masters his or her code declares ...
I am who I am	I am the author of my life
I am hardwired to react	I act, I don't react
I avoid risk and do whatever it takes to stay safe	I play to win
I avoid responsibility whenever I can	I am 100 percent responsible for my life
I hold on to grudges	I forgive unconditionally
I need to be right	I seek to understand
I don't challenge the status quo	I own my identity
I have limited potential	I never stop learning and growing

The average person who is run by a program believes ...	The extraordinary person who masters his or her code declares ...
I don't keep my commitments	*I am my word*
I don't control my destiny	*I live on purpose*

These ten declarations are the essential and complete code for leading an extraordinary life. They are the choices that will move you from a program designed almost exclusively to keep you safe to a code that gives you the freedom to shape the way you live. If you commit to mastering this code, your world will transform. You will unlock your full potential and live a life of joy, passion, and effectiveness. That is the promise of this book.

By turning the page, you are taking an important step on that journey. It is a journey that promises enormous reward, and I am honored and privileged to be your guide.

Let's go.

Chapter One
I Am the Author of My Life

We do not see the world as it is, we see the world as we are.
—The Talmud

Until you make the unconscious conscious, it will direct your life
and you will call it fate.
—Carl Gustav Jung

Your program's most fundamental rule is that your program cannot be changed. As you will learn, your program is designed to avoid risk and keep you safe. The last thing it wants is for you to tinker with it. This is perfect if your goal is simply to survive, to be a bystander in your own life. But if you're looking to lead an extraordinary life, this rule won't work. It is the first line of your program that you need to change.

~~{Rule: You are who you are}~~

I'm going to show you how to take the first step in mastering your code. To declare that you are the author of (not a bystander in) your life. First, we will explore the importance of awareness and why it is the precondition to authoring your life. You cannot change what you cannot see. Second, we will dive into the psychology of adult stage development—the notion that your awareness expands through distinct stages and that you can accelerate its development. Third, we will discuss the importance of the mind and the body, and the connection between the two. Finally, we will talk about how you can use language to create awareness—to see what you don't know (and don't even know that you don't know).

Why Awareness Is So Critical

Let's begin with your first lesson in awareness. One thing I can guarantee is that some part of your program is driving the way you are responding to the words in this book right now. I am almost certain that you are not aware of it. If you're like most people, you simply opened the book and began to read, unaware of the belief or assumption that is driving the meaning you give to each word on each page. And even if you're the exceptional person who is actually aware that this is going on, I am confident that you did not pause to examine the belief you brought to your reading or consciously choose the one that would best serve you.

I am going to invite you to do that right now. Take a moment to identify the assumption or belief you have about this book and write it down. Here are some examples to help you:

"If I'm not hooked after this first chapter, I'm going to stop reading."

"This reminds me of another book I read recently."

"I'm pretty sure I already know most of this stuff."

"I love this subject; I can't wait to dive in."

"There is no way a single book can teach me how to lead an extraordinary life."

Here's the thing about beliefs. They massively shape your actions and, therefore, the results you get in every part of your life. The good news is that once you have awareness of your beliefs, you can choose new ones. Choose a new belief and the actions that are available to you will expand. The greater the range of actions, the higher the probability of achieving the results you want. And what's amazing is that it doesn't matter whether your new belief is true or not. All that matters is whether the belief is going to serve you.

Consider the following story. Two shoe salesmen are dispatched by boat from London in the early 1900s to a developing country to determine if there is a market opportunity there. They arrive to see a massive population of people, none of whom are wearing shoes. The two men rush to the nearest telegraph office to send a message back to their company. The first sends the following: DISASTER. NO ONE HERE WEARS SHOES. I WILL BE ON NEXT BOAT HOME. The other salesman writes something different: GLORIOUS OPPORTUNITY. NO ONE HERE WEARS SHOES YET. SEND INVENTORY FAST.

Same circumstances, different outcomes. The only difference was the set of underlying beliefs each man held. The first saw the world as a place of scarcity. The second saw a world of abundance and possibility. Who was right? It doesn't really matter. What matters is that their programs determined the actions available to them. Different beliefs, different possibilities.

So if you start reading a book and you hold the belief "I already know a lot about what the author has written," the actions available to you will be those that confirm that belief. You will only pay attention to the content that seems new, and you will miss the nuance and distinction contained within the new content that you *believe* you already know.

Ask yourself whether the belief you just identified about this book will serve you, even if you're convinced it might be true. If your belief doesn't serve you, I would encourage you to leverage your awareness and *choose* a different belief. It might be "There's always something new that I can learn." From this belief, your reading will shift dramatically, and what you get out of the book will be enhanced in meaningful ways. You will be the author of your experience, not a passive recipient of it. And so it goes, as I hope to convince you, with all of life.

One of the most powerful explanations of awareness came from the late author David Foster Wallace in his 2005 commencement address to the graduating class at Kenyon College. In his speech, he tells the following story: Two young fish are swimming along one day. An older fish swims toward them and asks the younger fish, "Morning, boys, how's the water?" They say nothing. As soon as the older fish swims by, one of the younger fish asks the other in a bewildered way, "What the hell is water?"[1]

The point of the story is that you go through life like the younger fish, unaware that you are swimming through the waters of your biology, language, childhood experiences, and culture. These are the streams and currents that together shape, condition, and construct your program. Because you don't see them, you are run by them. To be the author of your life requires first that you become aware. Aware that you have a program and that it shapes everything about how you see yourself, others, and the world around you.

Without awareness, you simply act. Automatically and reflexively. Your mind creates an explanation, after the fact, that allows you to believe that you actually choose your response to situations. But more often than not, the actions you take are the product of the execution of the subconscious program that's running you. The great individuals throughout history have known this. They leveraged their awareness to master the practice of choosing beliefs that serve them. They weren't bystanders in their lives. They authored them.

How to Cultivate Awareness—The Science of Adult Stage Development

So if awareness is a precondition to being the author of your life, how do you cultivate it? Partly, awareness grows over time. The older you get, the more aware you become. How often have you told yourself, "If I only knew then what I know now . . ." This is because your awareness builds through distinct and predictable stages over time. To understand this phenomenon, we need to explore the domain of adult stage development. And to do so, it helps to start by looking at children.

Jean Piaget, one of the twentieth century's most influential psychologists, is responsible for much of our current understanding of childhood development. Piaget was born in 1896 in Neuchâtel, Switzerland. In the 1920s, he took an interest in understanding the development of knowledge, particularly in children. Over the course of the next few decades, he constructed and refined what has become the definitive theory of childhood development. Thanks to his pioneering research, we know that children go through distinct stages of intellectual and psychological growth, with their awareness proceeding through natural and predictable stages of increasing complexity.

To illustrate, consider the following study. Children are shown two identical empty beakers. They observe the first beaker being filled to a certain level with colored water. Then they are shown the second beaker being filled with colored water and are asked to say stop when both beakers have the same amount of water. The experimenter pours a bit of water from one to the other until the children agree that there is exactly the same amount of water in both. Finally, a third taller and thinner beaker is introduced. All of the water from the first beaker is poured into the third. Given the thinner size of the third beaker, the water rises to a higher level than in the second one. The children are then asked which of the two beakers (second or third) contains more water or whether they contain the same amount. Most children under the age of six will say the third beaker has more. By age seven and certainly by age eight, most children recognize that both beakers contain the same amount of water.

Piaget's pioneering work with this and other experiments helped us to understand what we now take for granted—that children go through distinct stages of development in how they make sense of the world around them. They become more aware as they grow. We know this from our own experience as parents of children and from being children ourselves.

I can recall my first time on an airplane. I was seven years old. I distinctly remember sitting at a window seat with my father directly to my left. I can still feel the tightness in my chest as we began to race down the runway, and then a drop in my stomach as we took off. Moments later, I opened the window shade and looked down at the ground several hundred feet below. To my seven-year-old mind, everything had shrunk in size. People looked like ants and cars seemed like miniature toys. I turned to my father in amazement and said, "Daddy, I can't believe it. All the people and the cars got tiny." It was only a couple of years later, on my next flight, that I magically had a different awareness of my own perception. I realized that of course the people and cars hadn't shrunk. How was it that my entire way of making meaning had shifted in such a short period of time? In the two years between flights, I had moved to a new and more complex stage of cognitive development.

What we now know—and have known for some time—is that cognitive development does not stop with the onset of adulthood. Adults, like children, go through distinct (albeit more difficult to detect) stages. Psychologist Robert Kegan's subject-object theory helps illustrate what happens as you move from one stage of adult development to the next.[2] According to this theory, when you are in a certain stage, you are *subject* to certain ways of making sense of the world. For example, you may orient your life around the need for external validation. You may not even be aware that you hold the belief that the opinions of others matter. In Kegan's view, you are *subject* to this belief. At some later point, you may actually be able to see that your need for external validation isn't just the way the world works. Rather, it is a belief that you have constructed. Once this happens, you are able to hold the belief as an *object* for reflection: *Does this need for external validation really serve me? Is it possible to act in a way that is not driven by what others think of me?* You can now allow for the possibility that what you think is at least as important, if not more so, than what others think. It doesn't mean that you completely disregard others; you're just no longer as driven by their opinions. You are now able to act and make sense of situations with greater freedom, nuance, and complexity. In other words, you have moved to the next stage of development.

For me, the impact of shifting from being driven by what others think of me to deciding whether or not what others think of me really matters was profound. I realized that what others think of me was neither objectively important nor unimportant. It was for me to decide. I realized I had been living my life subconsciously driven by the belief that I had to be liked.

```
{My Rule: It is important
        to be liked}
```

With this awareness and new choice, my range of actions expanded massively, and the results I began to get in life improved dramatically. One simple example was a new freedom to be much more direct in my conversations with people. I learned how to be frank in way that has built my relationships with people, even when the conversations were challenging.

In many ways, life is a succession of subject-object transitions, in which you move along different stages of increasing complexity in the way you make meaning of your circumstances and the actions you take. As you move from one stage to the next, you become aware of fundamental aspects of your program. This awareness allows you to choose to rewrite that part of it. In doing so, you are able to take actions and achieve results that you previously thought were unimaginable.

This brings some good news and some bad news. Let's start with the bad. Moving from one stage of development to the next can take a long time. Sometimes decades. And most people will plateau at a particular stage of development. Now here's the good news: mastering your code accelerates that development. The ten declarations in this book are designed to catalyze major shifts in your development that would otherwise take a long time to occur, if they occurred at all.

Before we get too far along, I want to arm you with an understanding of how the brain and body work together. This will allow you to understand and have more control over the complex nature of human behavior. You can then counteract the strong forces embedded in your culture and in the human condition that work against your capacity to shape your life.

Why It's So Important to Become a Student of the Brain

The brain is an amazing organ. It allows you to function by processing and filtering an unimaginable amount of input. Over the last two decades, we have learned an extraordinary amount about how the brain works and we continue to learn more every day. Yet there is so much we still don't know. Any attempt here to provide a simplified explanation of the brain's workings will undoubtedly do injustice to its complexity. Nevertheless, having a crude working idea of how the major areas of the brain work is essential to understanding how you are aware and what you can do to cultivate and strengthen that awareness.[3]

The information that you sense from outside your body—through your eyes, your ears, your nose, your skin—and from inside your body is sent to a part of the brain called the thalamus, located in the region of the brain called the limbic system. The thalamus then sends this information in two directions—down deeper into the subconscious limbic system to the amygdala and up to the prefrontal cortex (PFC). The PFC is where your conscious awareness resides. The amygdala has an advantage. It receives the information from the thalamus faster than the PFC does, and thus processes the information often before you are even consciously aware it has arrived.

The amygdala acts as sort of traffic cop, determining whether any of the information sent by the thalamus poses a threat to your survival. And it is not just about physical safety. Since we are social animals, human beings have developed a deep need to be included; being excluded from the tribe was tantamount to death. Threats to your psychological safety are thus just as important as risks to your physical well-being. The amygdala makes this safety determination by relying on the nearby hippocampus, allowing the brain to compare the new information being received to past experience and make a probability-based decision about what to do. If the amygdala senses danger, it signals the hypothalamus and brain stem to activate the autonomic nervous system and to release the hormone epinephrine. This is what we have come to know as the fight, flight, or freeze response. Your body moves into action, retreats, or shuts down depending on the stimulus and the signal. Because this all happens at the subconscious level, the response is essentially automatic. And because the information from the thalamus reaches the amygdala before it gets to the PFC, the more "rational" part of your brain doesn't have a chance to observe, evaluate, and choose how to respond. What is critical then is to strengthen the PFC's ability to down-regulate the amygdala. The more you can create space between the stimulus and the amygdala's response, the more you can have a choice about how you act and behave—and the more likely it will be that you will author your life.

While the role of the brain, and in particular the PFC, in cultivating awareness and choice is undoubtedly critical, the Western world is beginning to appreciate what the Eastern world has known for thousands of years— that awareness is not just developed top-down from the brain to the body. Rather, what may be equally or even more important is the body's bottom-up ability to regulate the brain.[4]

One of the most interesting hypotheses about the body's role in influencing the brain is polyvagal theory, first proposed in 1994 by Stephen Porges, a professor in the department of psychiatry at the University of North Carolina at Chapel Hill.[5] Polyvagal theory is concerned with the connection between the autonomic nervous system and the fight/flight/freeze response. The autonomic nervous system operates at the subconscious level. Its main purpose is to control bodily functions such as digestion, respiration, and heart rate. It is divided into two primary systems—the sympathetic and parasympathetic nervous systems. The sympathetic nervous system is the "get up and go" circuit that propels you into action. When your safety is threatened, it diverts blood from your stomach to your lungs and skeletal muscles, increases your heart rate, and dilates your pupils. Its counterpart, the parasympathetic nervous system, is responsible for rest and digestion. The vagus nerve is the longest nerve of the whole autonomic system, running from the stem of the brain all the way down to the lower organs.

According to the polyvagal theory, the vagus nerve is constantly receiving information from your body based on cues from your environment—facial expressions, tone of voice, etc.—to determine whether your social connections are at risk. The more coherent the interplay between the sympathetic and parasympathetic nervous systems, the more attuned you are to your surroundings and the more likely you are to correctly assess risk to your social safety. This is key. If you falsely conclude that your social connections are at risk, your sympathetic nervous system kicks in and triggers a fight/flight/freeze response. Because this response happens before the processing of the prefrontal cortex, you will react without any real awareness, and thus without the ability to consciously evaluate and choose your response.

How to Leverage Language in Strengthening Awareness

I want to comment briefly on the power of language to create awareness. While I'll get into this issue in more depth later in the book, for now, consider the amazing story of Helen Keller, who lost her ability to see and hear when she contracted a debilitating disease when she was nineteen months old. Helen recounted that, with hardly any access to language in her early years before the arrival of her teacher, Anne Sullivan, "I was like an unconscious clod of earth."[6] It was not until just before Helen's seventh birthday that Anne Sullivan introduced her to language, waking her from a state of nothingness to consciousness. As Helen tells the story, "I awoke to language, to knowledge, to love, to the usual concepts of nature, good, and evil. I was actually lifted from nothingness to human life."[7]

Language creates distinctions. By that, I don't mean the use of language to describe truth or fact, but to provide access to the possibility of discovering for yourself something that was previously unknown and that you didn't even know was unknown. Think about an arborist. Most have spent decades studying trees. They have developed a mastery of language within the domain of arboriculture that would boggle the mind of the average person. Imagine walking through a forest with an arborist. Do you think the forest you would experience would be the same forest that the arborist would experience? Most definitely not. In fact, one could argue that the two of you would be walking through two different worlds, two distinct realities. Yet the trees, shrubs, and vines that you both would be walking among would be exactly the same. The only difference would be the language and the distinctions that such language would provide. The forest would occur to you very differently than to the arborist due to the presence or absence of distinctions. If you think of awareness as the discovery of that which was previously unknown (and unknown that it was unknown), you will begin to see how language can create awareness.

You can observe the power of distinctions in everyday life. My wife and I will be driving back from a party or a wedding and invariably she will ask me, "Did you notice how beautiful the table centerpieces were?" Despite her asking me this question literally dozens of times, I always seem to answer somewhat sheepishly: "No. I didn't even notice the centerpieces."

One day I stopped and asked myself, "Why is it that my wife and I go to the same party, sit at the same table, talk to many of the same people, and come home with completely different experiences and recollections of the event?" The answer, of course, has to do with language and distinctions, and the awareness that they create. My wife has spent years in roles that have required her to master the domain of event planning. She has been the president of the board of trustees at our children's elementary school and the parents' associations of the middle and upper schools, served as chair of the annual auction a number of times, and put on and hosted countless fund-raisers. While I believe I have been a very supportive husband, my involvement in her work has been relatively minimal. As a result, she has gained fluency in a number of distinctions within the domain of event planning that I simply do not have. For example, she knows that pin-spot lighting allows guests to see what they're eating and to whom they're talking, which is distinct from more diffused lighting used to illuminate the social areas of the room. She also knows that the up lighting that accents columns and entries and exits is used to create ambiance and thematic effects but more importantly to identify key areas like bars and restrooms—two very related places in my experience. And she knows that shantung or satin table linens are distinct from basic cotton or polyester. They not only look better but are functionally superior. If you've ever put a plain white cotton napkin in your lap, you may remember the lint left on your clothes. No wonder that, with me not being aware of these distinctions, we can leave the same party having had very different experiences.

Extraordinary people are masters of the distinctions offered by language. They understand the capacity of language to create awareness. One of the promises of this book is to introduce you to new distinctions that will allow you to see yourself, others, and the world differently. I find that in my work with business leaders, one of the most powerful distinctions is one we have already discussed—the subject/object distinction. Most adults can intellectually grasp that they have beliefs, and even that they have beliefs or ways of seeing the world that are largely unexamined. What often creates breakthroughs for people, however, is the distinction between having beliefs and being driven by them (or being subject to them). You are now aware that you have been *subject* to a program that has been driving your life. With awareness, you can hold your program as *object*. Armed with this distinction and this new awareness, you will likely experience a newfound freedom of choice. No longer driven by unexamined parts of your program, you can be the master of your code and the author of your life.

***

OK, this is a lot to take in; let's make sense of it all. To lead an extraordinary life, you need to be the author of, not a bystander in, your life. To do that, you need to be aware that you have a program and to rewrite the parts that aren't serving you. You need to have a code that serves you, not a program that you serve. The problem is that whenever you receive a signal that you are threatened, your brain is designed to shut down your awareness and your ability to author your life. A threat signal can be real, like a rattlesnake. Or it can be a perceived threat to your social standing, like somebody rolling his eyes. In the latter case, you have a choice about how to act. To master your code, you have to know that you are going to receive signals like this all the time, be prepared for them, and take preemptive measures against letting your program respond automatically. To do this, you first must be aware. It requires that you declare you are the author of your life, not the product of your evolution.

Chapter Two
I Act, I Don't React

*Between stimulus and response there is a space. In that space is
our power to choose our response. In our response lies our growth
and our freedom.*
— Victor Frankl

Congratulations. You are the author of your life.
There's no turning back. Yet this is only a first
step in mastering your code; it is necessary but
not sufficient. The next part of your program to rewrite is
the belief that you are hardwired emotionally.

{Rule: ~~You are hardwired to react~~}

Like most of your deeply held beliefs, this is mostly
hogwash. I'll explain that, despite what you may think,
reality isn't some objective thing that exists out there and
happens to you; it's something you construct. As a result
of this insight, you will begin to see the power (and
responsibility) you have to reconstruct how you perceive
your circumstances so that you are in control of, not at
the effect of, the events in your life.

I'll begin by challenging some deeply held assumptions about how the world works. I'll then offer two effective practices that will help you start mastering being the
actor, not a reactor, in your life. With these practices, you
will begin to intentionally and regularly examine your
beliefs and optimize your physiology, so that your brain
and body begin to serve you, not the other way around.

They will become the foundation of your mastery, and we will return to them throughout the book. Finally, we will explore the importance of practicing.

Remember, your program was designed to keep you safe. It does not want you to change. If you want to master your life and lead it according to the code you create, you have to be willing to take a hard look at who you think you are.

Addressing (and Questioning) Two Fundamental Myths About Human Behavior

One of the most important skills I hope you develop and deepen as you read this book is the master skill of challenging and shattering myths. As you will see in later chapters, myths are everywhere. They serve to preserve precious cognitive capacity, so that you don't have to think too hard. This is great for the average person, as myths always contain some element of truth and can be a helpful guide to making sense of the complexity of the world. But a master critically challenges prevailing myths. Not in some negative, cynical sense. Rather, a master has the courage to question deeply held beliefs of her own and of society more broadly. The master thinks critically because she knows that she (and only she) has the responsibility for her own life.

Over the past two decades, there has been a quiet revolution in the fields of psychology and neuroscience challenging two fundamental assumptions. The first is that humans are hardwired to experience emotions and that emotions happen automatically. Unless you're a saint, if you've been honked at by a rude driver, you will have seen this firsthand. You will have experienced reacting in a way that feels completely automatic (and likely regrettable). This is certainly what seems to be happening. The proximity between stimulus (the honk) and reaction (anger) is so close that your perception was that you had no choice but to react in a certain way. To make sense of this experience, you likely have attributed this phenomenon to the myth that humans are emotionally hardwired.

This is understandable. Early humans who were able to band together effectively increased their likelihood of survival. Evolution favored traits that let people be accepted by and remain part of the clan. In essence, getting excluded from the tribe was an almost certain death sentence. As a result, your brain has evolved to recognize threats to your social status and to respond in ways that protect you from risk to your psychological safety. In fact, brain scans show that when you feel excluded or rejected, the part of your brain associated with physical pain—the anterior cingulate cortex—lights up. Hence, as we saw in chapter one, when someone looks at you a certain way or makes a disparaging remark, your amygdala is triggered and institutes a fight/flight/freeze response, releasing the hormone epinephrine and instigating a series of physiological responses. This reaction, known as the amygdala hijack, in turn impairs your most sophisticated mental capabilities—your ability to think rationally, to be creative, to problem solve, to exercise self-control. What started out as an essential survival adaptation—to keep you safe from physical harm or to keep you included in the tribe—has become a major limitation to effectiveness in modern-day life.

So while there may be something to the notion of hardwiring, the truth is far more nuanced and interesting. Your brain is a prediction machine, continuously comparing new stimuli to past experience and making guesses about what action your body should take based on those comparisons. Beginning in early infancy, your brain begins to construct rules or beliefs for each category of experience, and they get embedded in your program. Over time, these rules solidify, and you think it is just the way things are—the way you are wired. Driver honking at you equals someone treating you unfairly, which means you must be angry.

One of the leading researchers in this area, Lisa Feldman Barrett, has arrived at a profound and revolutionary conclusion challenging the myth that humans are hardwired:

> Our emotions aren't built-in, waiting to be revealed. They are *made*. By *us*. We don't *recognize* emotions or *identify* emotions: we *construct* our own emotional experiences, and our perceptions of others' emotions, on the spot, as needed, through a complex interplay of systems. Human beings are not at the mercy of mythical emotion circuits buried deep within animalistic parts of our highly evolved brain: we are architects of our own experience.[8]

The second fundamental assumption being challenged is the view that what you perceive through your senses—primarily sight and sound—dictates the way you feel. In reality, it is mostly the other way around. We touched on this notion in chapter one with the introduction of polyvagal theory—the idea that your central nervous system is constantly scanning your internal state to detect physiological markers that suggest potential threats to your social safety. You continuously experience countless sensations in your body—the result of your glucose levels, breathing rate, lack of sleep, etc. Your brain's process of registering and integrating changes in these sensations is known as interoception. Interoception influences what external sensory input you pay attention to. If sleep-deprived and hungry, you will experience the same situation completely differently than you would if well-rested and fed. Again, Barrett does a wonderful job of summarizing this for us:

> *You construct the environment in which you live.* You might think about your environment as existing in the outside world, separate from yourself, but that's a myth. You (and other creatures) do not simply find yourself in an environment and either adapt or die. You construct your environment—your reality—by virtue of what sensory input from the physical environment your brain selects; it admits some as information and ignores some as noise. And this selection is intimately linked to interoception.[9]

The implications of this paradigm shift in understanding human behavior are massive. The sum of your genetics, childhood experiences, culture, neurophysiology (including the anatomy of your brain and, more importantly, your physiological state) all help shape your program and, in turn, how you behave. Your brain uses the rules of your program to make predictions about what actions are most appropriate for any given stimulus. This understanding is revolutionary, and it's good news. While it is certainly understandable to feel as if certain behaviors are automatic, you nevertheless have the capacity to control every response to every situation. The question now becomes what you can do to master your code (including your physiology) so that the actions you take are more consistent with the choices you would like to make. Since you are truly the architect and author of your experience, you have the possibility (and dare I say responsibility) to create the conditions that will allow you to construct a different way of perceiving and reacting to your circumstances. The bad news? No more excuses!

Let's take the car honking example. Suppose you have always admired (and, at the same time, found hard to understand) a friend of yours who has the uncanny ability to react calmly when another driver honks rudely. Perhaps this friend always seems to offer a possible reason for the rude driver's behavior, like he's late to pick up his child or is rushing to get to the hospital to see to a sick relative. While you admire your friend's ability, there is no way you could imagine yourself exhibiting such extraordinary self-control. You're not even sure you would want to. In fact, every time a driver honks at you, your heart beats faster, you get flushed, you become angry, and you might fantasize about what you would do to that person in a dark alley. Perhaps you honk back or, worse, start tailgating the person "just to show them." Whatever your version of being pissed off looks like, it certainly doesn't resemble the friend you admire. So you begin to justify your actions. You may attribute your reaction to hardwiring. You may shift responsibility for your behavior to the other driver—she was at fault or deserved being honked back at. And you would leave it at that. Most of us do. Because, after all, it's just the way it is, the way we're wired. Or so we think.

With a different understanding of human behavior, however, there is the possibility (and responsibility) of choosing something different. Your "automatic" reaction may not be so automatic after all. This conditioned response of anger to someone who treats you unfairly is not something innate, not a function of the way your brain evolved. Rather, your response is a social construction, every bit as real and true as genetics and neuroanatomy, but constructed nonetheless. By social construction, I mean that the belief or rule is something that you learned as an infant or child and that was reinforced through your culture and ongoing experiences. Because it is constructed, it can be reconstructed. If you so choose, you can rewrite your rules for how you respond to your environment. This is what someone who masters his code and leads an extraordinary life does.

Recall the subject/object distinction discussed in the last chapter. You can either be *subject* to the rude driver and *react* subconsciously in a way that causes you to release the hormone epinephrine and dysregulate your autonomic nervous system, which distracts you and generally causes you to be unhappy and suffer. Or you can hold the action of the driver as *object* and choose to *respond* with empathy (or even indifference) toward the driver and equanimity regarding the situation. I'm not suggesting one action is necessarily better than the other, only that you get to choose. Not to be too dramatic, but you have a choice to be a slave to or a master of your emotions. Someone who controls their circumstances and decides their actions, or someone who is powerless and lets events control him. The only thing that truly gets in your way of authoring a different response is the social construction that to do so seems unnatural.

{Rule: ~~When someone treats you unfairly, you should be angry~~}

So the real question is, How do you reconstruct your rule around the situation so that someone being rude to you doesn't necessarily require an angry emotional response?

How to Master Your Emotions

If you want to be the master of your emotions, there are two fundamental practices. The first is to intentionally *examine and choose your beliefs.*[10] *There are four steps to this practice.* You have already been introduced to and are beginning to master the first step—awareness. You now have a set of distinctions, such as subject/object and social construction, that allow you to see that your automatic behavior isn't truly automatic. You are now aware that you have beliefs, that they are constructed, and that they can be reconstructed. Sorry, no more excuses.

Step two is to name the part of your program that underlies your behavior. In the case of your reaction to the "rude" driver, your belief might have been "All people who are rude are bad." Or "There is no excuse for rude behavior." Or "People who behave badly need to be taught a lesson." Finally, you likely have the rule "All people who honk for any longer than a tap are rude." Whatever belief or rule you may be holding, it is likely to be subconscious and it is certainly something that you have constructed over time. It is part of your program, and it has been there so long that you consider it to be pretty obvious and uncontroversial. You don't see it as part of your program, but rather just the way the world works.

Step three is to examine the particular belief that is driving your behavior. The only way to act, as opposed to react, is to relax the grip your beliefs and rules have on you. The best way to accomplish this is to submit your beliefs to honest examination. You might begin by asking, "What happens inside me when I have this particular belief?" When you believe "There is no excuse for rude behavior" and you encounter someone you think is rude, you likely will immediately feel something in your body. Your chest may get tight. Your throat may constrict. You may get a knot in your stomach. You may get flushed with redness or heat. You may experience all of these sensations. If you're not paying attention to your body, forget about being the actor in your life. Your body is telling your brain what to pay attention to. So you have to both observe what's happening in your body and then sit with, and breathe through the sensation until you have restored a level of balance. This practice is called getting grounded or centered or self-regulated.

Once you're centered, the fourth and final step is to really question the belief. You will want to see where it is that the belief isn't true. You might ask yourself, "Where can I see that the driver wasn't being rude?" If you slow down and let go of your attachment to being certain and right, there is no shortage of possibilities. The driver may have honked longer than she intended. Or she may have been honking at someone else. She may not have even honked at all—it might have been someone else. How many times have you honked at someone only to feel bad or to have been misunderstood? The point is, if you really try, you can find several reasons to begin to question your belief. After seeing where your belief might be untrue, next find where that belief might equally apply to you. In the case of the rude driver, you might ask, "Where is *my* behavior or thinking rude?" The answer to that question is typically amusing and revealing. Middle finger, fantasies of a dark alley, your internal narrative. If you're like me, there's no shortage of evidence pointing to where your thinking and behavior might have been less than polite.

It is here where most people get stuck. When asked to question their deeply held beliefs, they can become resistant and defensive. And this is understandable. For example, it may seem preposterous or offensive to suggest that rude behavior is excusable or to start seeing where you might be rude. The point here is not to deny the truth of the belief that you are questioning. Of course, you don't simply want to excuse rude behavior or deny the reality that rude behavior has consequences. Rather, the point is to soften the attachment to your belief.

I like to use the metaphor of the golf swing. If you've ever tried to learn how to play golf, my apologies. It can be the most frustrating, counterintuitive experience—particularly if you take it up as an adult, like I did. One of the things you learn when you are being introduced to golf is that holding the golf club tight doesn't help you hit the ball farther or with greater accuracy. In fact, a grip that is too tight will force the other muscles in your arms to tighten and thereby slow down the swing of the club. It will also take away the feel you need to have as you strike the ball. On the other hand, hold the club too loosely and you will have no control. What you are doing when you examine your beliefs is loosening your grip enough to allow for more fluidity and give yourself the capacity to notice different things and take different action. When you loosen the grip on your beliefs, you have more room to choose and consider alternatives without completely abandoning your core beliefs. You might begin to ask, "Does holding this belief serve me?" Or "Can I see where holding this belief is limiting my effectiveness?"

The second fundamental practice is leveraging and optimizing your body. Recall that one of the fundamental assumptions that we have challenged is the notion that the brain tells the body what to do. As you now know, the relationship between the brain and body is bidirectional.

In fact, I would argue that the body influences the brain more than the other way around. Your physiological state drives what you focus on and what meaning you give to your circumstances, which in turn determine the actions you take and the results you get. The simplest way to appreciate this phenomenon is to try the following exercise right now. Breathe deeply, put your arms in the air, and smile as if you are the happiest you've ever been. While maintaining this state, try to think a negative thought. You can't. It's impossible.

What's going on here? Your body, through the combination of your posture, facial expressions, and breath, sends an unmistakable signal to your brain. The way you hold your body—your posture—can powerfully influence how you interpret your environment. If your legs are crossed and your hands folded in front of your abdomen, guess what message that sends to your brain? You got it. Your posture is telling your brain that you are guarding against a potential predator and protecting your vital organs. With this posture and attendant signal, your brain will narrow its focus so that you pay attention only to potential risk and danger. It won't allow much room for you to notice much else. And your capacity to choose how to respond will be massively constrained, given the shutdown of the prefrontal cortex that accompanies a fear state.

The same thing is true with your facial expressions. You may have been taught to believe that your moods and emotions trigger your expressions. If you're happy, you smile. If you're sad or angry, you frown. The research suggests that the opposite is equally true. There are now a number of studies, for example, demonstrating that patients who receive Botox injections in the frown lines around the mouth or in the forehead furrows experience less anxiety and depression. When you smile, your body is letting your brain know that things are safe. In turn, what you pay attention to and how you interpret events shift dramatically. As do your actions and results.

Finally, what may be most important is your breathing. This makes sense. The next time you find yourself anxious, angry, or frustrated, pause for a moment and focus on your breath. What you will undoubtedly notice is that you have literally stopped breathing. What signal do you think your body is sending to your brain in that moment? Hint: "You are going to die shortly!" As a result, your brain will immediately go into survival mode. It will interpret the fact that you stopped breathing in response to a slight by your spouse or an offhand comment by your colleague as a threat to your psychological safety. You will then act subconsciously following your program, likely in a manner that isn't effective. By simply taking a few deep breaths, you will be able to induce a totally different physiological state. One that allows you to see more data, to interpret your surroundings in a totally different way, and to be able to choose how you behave.

As you begin to practice using your physiology, you will notice that your performance in life will take off. You will have more energy. You will have more control of your moods. You will tend to see possibility rather than obstacles. Your level of certainty and confidence will grow.

What is equally true, but less obvious, is that your physiology will impact the physiology of others. Human beings, like most mammals, mirror and mimic one another. Mirroring is a way for people to build rapport, which is key to establishing social connection, a fundamental human need. If you've ever watched two people seated and talking to each other, you will observe this phenomenon in action. Over time, as they attune to each other, their postures, facial expressions, and even breathing patterns begin to match. Even more interesting, perhaps, is what's known as co-regulation, in which the rhythm of a person's nervous system will begin to sync with the nervous systems of those around her. If you are in any position of influence—a parent, a leader, a teacher—think about the impact your physiology can have on those who depend on you. This is a big part of my work with leaders. If you want to be an effective leader, your job is to create conditions that unlock the maximum potential of those you are leading. This can't happen if you are not managing and optimizing your own physiology first.

Finally, I am sure you know the importance of diet, sleep, and exercise and their connection to performance. I will be the first to emphasize how important those three ingredients are to living an extraordinary life. And yet, true masters know there will be times when they are hungry, sleep-deprived, or out of shape. Or maybe even all three. It is at those times—when the body is depleted—that true masters know how to manage and optimize their physiology. While they honor their bodies by eating well, sleeping, and exercising regularly, they don't use the inevitable lack of any of these as an excuse for not choosing how to skillfully interpret and respond to their environment. This is now your task. Your commitment must be to use your posture, facial expressions, and breath in an intentional manner. In a way that allows you to choose to be the actor in your life, not just a bystander in it.

Practice Is Everything

You may be thinking, "In the split second of time between someone being rude to me and my reaction, there is no way I can go through all these steps." And, of course, you are right. Again, the golf analogy. When I was learning to play golf, each time I struck the ball on the range, I would spend at least a minute making sure my setup was right. Was there the correct amount of distance between my legs? Was my stance in line with where I wanted to hit the ball? Was I standing too close to or too far from the ball? Did I have the club properly placed in my hands so that the face would be neither too open nor too closed? And, yes, was I holding the club too tightly or too loosely? Today, while I hardly play golf and am only an average player at best, I can walk up to a ball and within seconds set up and strike it with relative ease. The few years I spent taking lessons and hitting practice balls on the range allowed me to move forward in the conscious/competence spectrum.

Before I even started playing the sport, I was *subconsciously incompetent*. I had no idea what was involved and had this vague, contemptuous notion that I would be a good golfer if I simply tried. I mean, how hard can it be to hit a small, stationary ball on the ground? As I took up the sport, I gradually became *consciously incompetent*. I was increasingly aware of how challenging the sport was and how difficult it was for me. For about a year, I struggled to get to even a basic level of proficiency where I wouldn't embarrass myself or, worse yet, injure someone else with a stray ball. About two years into taking lessons and practicing regularly, I gradually became *consciously competent*. I had to think hard about what I was doing, but things were coming more naturally to me. Today, I straddle the line between consciously incompetent and consciously competent. In contrast, a good friend of mine, who has played all his life, can, after a long time off from the game and without any warm-up, hit the ball effortlessly. He is *subconsciously competent*.

Hitting a golf ball is so ingrained and embodied for him that he doesn't even have to think about what he is doing.

So it is with questioning your beliefs and optimizing your physiology. These are practices in which it takes time to gain competence or mastery. Some readers, particularly those for whom the idea of questioning beliefs is new, may be subconsciously incompetent most of the time. If you commit to the practice of questioning your beliefs, you will spend quite a while going back and forth between subconscious and conscious incompetence. But, make no mistake about it, you will be incompetent! Over time, as with any practice, if you are diligent, you will begin to experience a conscious competence. A driver will honk at you. You will notice your anger. You may even begin to sense it in your body. You may perhaps have an internal narrative running about how inexcusable the driver's behavior is and how the world would be a better place without jerks like them in it. But you will be able to step back and observe, to hold as object the experience you are having. You will be able to reframe the belief, turn it around, and allow for just a bit of room to respond in a way that is truly a choice. And you will leverage your posture, facial expression, and breath to support you. This is an essential skill and discipline if you are to truly master your code.

To master anything in life, you first have to master the discipline of practice. To do so, it helps to understand the phenomenon of neuroplasticity. For much of the first half of the twentieth century, scientists assumed that brain structure evolved during childhood and adolescence but became fixed at adulthood. It was not until the early 1970s that they began to discover that the brain is constantly changing, even late into life, as a result of behavior and environment. Donald Hebb captured the essence of this phenomenon with his famous quote "Neurons that fire together, wire together." Essentially, Hebb was describing neuroplasticity, the idea that repeated neural activity strengthens the connections between neurons over time. In turn, those strengthened connections make it more likely that the resulting behavior will occur with greater ease. This was a revolutionary finding. The evidence accumulated since then indicates overwhelmingly that with practice, new behaviors become more habitual because they are supported by new, strengthened neural structures. The more you practice questioning your beliefs and managing your physiology, the easier and more habitual it will be to engage in your desired behaviors. Subconscious competence will come from the intentional, deliberate, and repetitive practice of new behaviors. With practice, you will literally begin to experience a new reality. You will act, not react. You will be the master of your behavior.

Chapter Three
I Play to Win

I don't live in the past. I don't play my old records for that reason. I make a statement, then move on to the next.
— Prince

Being human is a condition that requires a little anesthesia.
— Freddie Mercury (in Bohemian Rhapsody)

Y ou have now chosen to author your life. You understand that you are not hardwired to react. That you can (and have the responsibility to) choose how you act in any situation. By now, you are probably beginning to see that the deepest and most hidden parts of your program were written in your childhood years, when you were most psychologically vulnerable. Many of your deep-seated beliefs were formed largely in response to traumatic events. The trauma may have been relatively minor, like being teased as a child or reprimanded by a parent. In other cases, the trauma may have been severe. Whatever their source, at the time of their construction, these compensatory beliefs served an incredibly important purpose—to keep you safe.

{Rule: Avoid risk and do whatever it
takes to stay safe}

By the time you're an adult, however, these beliefs have mostly outlived their usefulness. Your job now is to take a hard look at the outdated parts of your program that continue to run your life. To debug your program and rewrite the parts that were designed to keep you safe as a child but that may no longer serve you.

Here's the problem: the parts of your program that were designed to keep you safe, what I call "survival strategies," have worked extremely well. So well that they are incredibly difficult to give up. And there's a kicker: the more traumatic your past, the more embedded these survival strategies are in your program and the more difficult they will be to change.

To choose to play to win in life, then, you must become a master of your past. You have to know what you're up against. You must understand the psychological and neurobiological connections between your past and who you are today. Make no mistake: I do not believe your past constrains who you can become and how you can live your life. But, unless you master your past, you will remain a prisoner of it. In this chapter, I will give you the tools to master the past. You will be able to see how much it currently controls you. You will be in a position to own it and to declare that you will no longer be imprisoned by it. You will no longer play not to lose. You will finally be able to say, "I play to win."

I'll begin with a review of a central theory underlying human behavior called attachment theory. If you choose to master your code, you need to have a general understanding of how this works. We'll then explore the related effects of trauma on your development. The more traumatic your past, the more your program will be written to keep you safe. The more your program is written to keep you safe, the more difficult it will be to rewrite it so you can play to win. I will offer you an exercise to identify the parts of your program that were constructed in response to trauma, and a way to rewrite those parts so that you can move from being run by a survival program to creating a code that will let you thrive. I'll conclude by challenging two myths concerning the role of genetics and the nature of addiction and offering a new paradigm for understanding human behavior.

As you read this chapter, I encourage you to dig deep into the material. Read the chapter like a master. Question your thinking. And continue to ask yourself how these concepts apply to you and to others in your life.

***

My quest to really master my past began when I became the CEO of a large career college serving more than thirteen thousand adult learners in largely vocational programs in multiple campuses across a number of states. Almost every one of our students had suffered some form of hardship that had become an obstacle to his or her success in traditional institutions of learning. Our industry was plagued by abysmal results. A typical career college was lucky if it could graduate 25 percent of its students. Public community colleges, on average, fared even worse. I was determined that our organization would achieve dramatically better results. And I was convinced that we could.

To do this, I first had to really understand our students and understand teaching. I had a slight problem, though: I had never taught before. I couldn't hope to reinvent an industry I really didn't know much about. So I decided I was not only going to lead this organization, but I was going to do so by example. During the day I was CEO. At night, I was a college instructor. I began by teaching an introductory class called Success 100 designed for first-quarter, first-year students. It was focused on teaching academic, career, and personal strategies for success. I wanted to do everything in my power to create an extraordinary experience for my students. To do that, I needed to learn as much as I could about the science of learning and human behavior. In the two months before the start of that first quarter, I dove in deep and began to devour books on psychology, human development, philosophy, neuroscience, biology, learning science, and childhood development. Little did I know that I was about to embark on a learning and development journey that would become the driving purpose and passion in my life.

Your First Few Years: The Science Behind Attachment Theory

It was at this time that I learned about attachment theory. First proposed by British psychologist John Bowlby in the 1960s, attachment theory asserts that an infant's development is greatly impacted by the presence or absence of a strong emotional and physical attachment to a primary caregiver. In the decades following Bowlby's groundbreaking work, researchers began to uncover the neurobiological basis for this phenomenon.

In one famous study, rat pups were observed immediately after birth. Some were regularly licked and groomed by their mother, others were not. The researchers studied the effects of this maternal behavior and discovered that the rat pups who were licked and groomed regularly were much healthier emotionally and mentally when they reached adulthood than the pups who were not. In fact, the licking and grooming actually reshaped the development of the pups' brains. The researchers then went one step further, placing the neglected pups with foster mother rats who licked and groomed. The results were exactly the same. The pups who were licked and groomed, even by a foster mother, performed better and were healthier in adulthood. This study raised a profound question: Could the presence or absence of a loving, attentive caregiver actually affect the development of the human brain? I began to think about my students and their childhood experiences. And I began to think about my own. What was the impact of early adverse experiences on the lives of my students? On my life?

It turns out that the impact of your early childhood environment is significant. Decades of research have established an undeniable connection between the presence or absence of a secure environment and a child's development. One particularly pioneering doctor stands out: Vincent Felitti. In 1985, Dr. Felitti was serving as the chief of Kaiser Permanente's Department of Preventative Medicine in San Diego. At the time, it was the largest medical evaluation center in the world, serving more than fifty thousand patients each year. It had a national reputation for large-scale, innovative approaches to health care. One of the department's key programs was an obesity clinic, which Dr. Felitti had started in 1980. Designed for people who were one hundred to six hundred pounds overweight, the clinic produced remarkable results, with the majority of patients losing more than one hundred pounds in a matter of months.

Yet, despite this success, the clinic experienced a more than 50 percent dropout rate. Dr. Felitti was baffled. Why would patients who were successful in losing significant amounts of weight leave the program? To figure out why, Dr. Felitti took it upon himself to personally interview hundreds of patients who had dropped out. He developed a standard set of questions to ask each patient. After the first few weeks of interviews, he was

no closer to an answer than when he first started. And
then, in a classic scientific "mistake," Dr. Felitti mis-
spoke and asked one patient how much she *weighed*
when she was first sexually active, when he had meant
to ask her how old she was. The new question elicited a
surprising and alarming response from the patient: forty
pounds. It turned out that she had been sexually abused
by her father beginning at age four. The doctor asked
other patients the same thing and uncovered a history of
childhood sexual abuse in the majority of those he interviewed. He began to hypothesize that perhaps the com-
pulsion to overeat was an addictive response designed
to soothe or numb the effects of the trauma his patients
had experienced as children. No wonder that the clinic
was experiencing such a high dropout rate. Successful
patients were leaving the program so that they could
return to overeating as a way of soothing the continued
effects of their unresolved trauma.

Understanding the Effects of Trauma

From that initial hypothesis, Dr. Felitti set out to identify the effects of childhood trauma in general. Over the
course of the next two years, he and his staff surveyed
more than seventeen thousand patients. They divided
childhood trauma into ten separate categories. The first
three were forms of abuse: sexual, physical, and verbal.
Two were forms of neglect: physical and emotional. The
remaining traumas were forms of family dysfunction: a
parent with mental illness, an alcoholic parent, a mother
who had been a victim of domestic violence, a family
member who had been incarcerated, and loss of a parent through divorce or abandonment. They developed a
scoring system known as ACE, for "adverse childhood
experience." For every type of reported trauma (regard-

less of degree and frequency), the patient would score one point on a maximum scale of ten. For example, if a patient had suffered physical abuse, had a mother who had been a victim of domestic violence, and had been separated from a parent through divorce, that patient would score a three on the ACE test.

The results were astounding. Two-thirds of the patients surveyed had experienced at least one type of adverse childhood experience. Of those, almost nine out of ten experienced two or more ACEs. The effects of the experiences were troubling and undeniable. Patients who had four or more ACEs, for example, were twice as likely to be smokers, twelve times more likely to have attempted suicide, seven times more likely to be an alcoholic, and ten times more likely to have injected street drugs. Overall, people with high ACE scores were more likely to be violent, to have more marriages, more broken bones, more drug prescriptions, more depression, more autoimmune diseases, and more absences from work.

On a personal note, my ACE score is a four. My father was incarcerated for short periods of time throughout my childhood. I was estranged from my mother, who suffered from alcohol and drug abuse, during my teenage years. And my father suffered from severe bouts of anxiety. Yet, for as long as I can remember, I felt loved and cared for, particularly by my father. I certainly am aware that my childhood experiences have had an effect on me and have shaped the way I see the world, but I have escaped the more serious consequences of severe childhood trauma. I am thankful that I have not suffered from substance abuse, depression, mental illness, or other serious health issues. Was it possible that the continuous attuned caring from my father served as an effective antidote to the traumatic nature of my childhood? Could

the love and safety I felt from him have protected me
from the consequences of a volatile and, at times, unsafe
environment? It's something I will never know for sure.

What we do know with greater and greater certainty,
however, is the following: adverse childhood experiences (including adverse in utero experiences) create
a stressed response in the fetus and child. When you
experience stress, your body automatically releases the
hormone epinephrine that activates your central nervous
system to prepare your body to fight, flee, or freeze. This
evolutionary response is highly effective. It has allowed
the human species to survive. Yet, when your stress-re-
sponse system becomes overactive, which is what happens to a child who suffers repeated traumatic experiences, your body becomes flooded with hormones. What
is beneficial in small, infrequent doses becomes toxic
in large, frequent measures, particularly for infants and
children. The most immediate and negative result is the
retardation of neurological development, particularly the
growth of the prefrontal cortex, which (as we learned in
chapter one) is responsible for self-regulation and executive function. Very young children are at the highest risk,
since neurological development occurs with greatest
intensity in the first two years of life. The one protection against the toxic effects of childhood trauma? You
guessed it. The presence of an attuned, loving caretaker.

Something else very important happens with trauma
beyond the neurobiological effects. During a traumatic
event, you subconsciously add lines to your program.
You form beliefs and rules that are designed to ensure
that you never experience the trauma again. The more
severe the trauma, the more deeply ingrained the beliefs
and rules, and the harder they are to rewrite. Think
back to when you were a kid, when you experienced an

event where your sense of belonging and social safety was threatened. You might have been teased, or bullied, or excluded from the group. Regardless of the severity of the event, you made a commitment in that moment to do whatever it took to avoid being in that situation again. This became your survival strategy, a sort of super rule that drove (and likely continues to drive) how you behave to ensure you remain psychologically safe.

There are essentially three categories of survival strategies.[11] We all possess, to some degree or another, a mix of all three, but we usually have a dominant one. The first is a *belonging* strategy. A person with a dominant belonging strategy will operate out of a deep commitment to being liked, to belonging, or to being included. For this person, to belong is to be safe. The second is a *distancing* strategy. The person with this orientation seeks safety by maintaining some sense of separateness and distance. He or she will be committed to being right, to being smart, to being above it all. Finally, there is the *controlling* strategy. These people find safety through achieving and are committed to winning, to results, or to being perfect.

Here's the thing about survival strategies. They are extremely powerful. They are deeply embedded in your program. In fact, you likely so strongly identify with the strategy itself that you cannot imagine life without it. You are completely driven by it and likely don't even realize it. Survival strategies work incredibly well if you're committed to playing not to lose. If you choose to play to win, however, these strategies won't get you there.

Let me explain with a personal example. I was born in London, England, and came to the United States when I was seven years old. Being a child with an English accent in Southern California in the 1970s was, to put it mildly, not cool. I remember being teased for my accent and I remember how painful it was to feel excluded.

{My Rule: Do whatever it takes
to not be different}

I also went to a new school every year until I was twelve. Every year there would be another set of kids who I had to make sure liked me as quickly as possible. I was totally committed to not being teased and not being different.

{My Rule: Whatever you do,
make sure that others like you}

While I wasn't conscious of it at the time, I now understand that my survival strategy was to do whatever it took to be included. It was a belonging strategy. And the belief that I constructed at age seven was "I am safe if I am liked." So I did everything I could to become like-able. And I got really good at it—so good that I ceased to see being liked as separate from who I was. For a long time, I was committed to being liked because not to be liked was not to be. It was essential to my social and psychological survival.

This strategy served me really well. I was popular at school. My teachers liked me. My colleagues at work were drawn to partner with me. Clients specifically requested that I work on their projects. But the strategy also had significant limitations. Because of my compulsive, self-identifying relationship to the need to be liked, there was no possibility of being any other way. For many years I found it really hard to engage in difficult conversations, deliver tough feedback, or frankly do anything that could cause someone not to like me. While

I was a good mentor, I deprived people who worked with me of an honest assessment of their performance. Because I was so likeable, I actually made it difficult for people to give me the kind of direct feedback I needed, and I missed out on opportunities to learn. I was playing not to lose, and I compromised my growth and my relationships with others.

Take a moment right now and identify which survival strategy is most dominant for you. Is it belonging, distancing, or controlling? What belief or rule do you hold as part of that strategy? For example, if you have a belonging strategy, your belief could be "I need to be accepted." If it's a distancing strategy, it might be "I need to be right." Once you've identified the belief, list all the ways this belief has served and protected you. Where have you and others benefited from this belief in your life? Then list all the ways this survival strategy limits your effectiveness. Where does it hold you back? Where have you been playing it safe?

Identifying, examining, and shifting your survival strategies—and you have many of them—is a critical skill. To play to win and lead an extraordinary life requires that you recognize and deal with the survival rules you have written over time. You will begin to notice how many you have. How they have protected you and how much you have benefited from them. You will also begin to see their limitations, where they inhibit your effectiveness and how they impact your relationships with others. I encourage you to begin to experiment with your dominant strategy. This will be massively transformational for you. You can then experiment with more and more of your survival beliefs. Over time, you will see your life change. No longer imprisoned by your past, you will be shaping your life and finally playing to win.

A New Paradigm for Understanding Human Behavior

Before we move on, let's zoom out for a moment and consider some statistics. In the United States alone, approximately two-thirds of adults report suffering from at least one adverse childhood experience. Almost one in four adults reports three or more ACEs. One in four children will experience an ACE before his or her fourth birthday. Sexual assault statistics vary, but research suggests that one in three women will experience sexual abuse in her lifetime. According to the World Health Organization, more than three hundred million people suffer from depression worldwide. Seven percent of Americans suffered a major depressive episode in the past year alone. Finally, almost 10 percent of the U.S. population meets the diagnostic criteria for drug or alcohol use disorder. Substance abuse is estimated to cost the United States $740 billion annually.[12]

These are alarming statistics. And they don't seem to be getting any better with time. Given the decades of overwhelming research pointing to the adverse effects of childhood trauma on adult behavior, one could reasonably expect a dramatic and different response from public policy officials and health care professionals. One that focuses more of our resources on the underlying conditions of suffering and treats the symptoms with a more nuanced understanding of the complexity of the problem. Unfortunately, this has not happened. Why not?

I think it is due to a dominant worldview—a myth perhaps—that owes its origins to the philosopher René Descartes and his scientific bedfellow Isaac Newton. The writings and discoveries of these two men (among many others of course) gave rise to a new way to conceptualize the world. No longer mystical in nature, the world followed a set of observable and predictable universal laws. The machine became its guiding metaphor. Logic and proof became the currency. And a new way of thinking emerged—one that was much more mechanistic, linear, and rational. The Scientific Revolution that took place after the Renaissance gave rise to what is now known as the Newtonian-Cartesian paradigm.

Most of Western civilization's ideologies, policies, and cultures have been shaped by this dominant paradigm. The modern world is conditioned by a strong need for proof supplied through objective data. We have a dominant bias to explain phenomena through cause and effect. And we struggle unrelentingly (and often erroneously) to reduce the complexity of life into easier to understand bite-size pieces. This worldview has resulted in some remarkable breakthroughs in our understanding of human behavior. It has also meaningfully constrained our thinking as a result of encouraging a strong preference for mechanistic theories at the expense of more dynamic, complex ways of understanding human beings. One such theory that has been dominant for some time is genetic determinism. In part, it asserts that much of human behavior can be explained by an individual's genetic makeup. The theory goes further, suggesting that by understanding the genetic code, we will someday be able to find a specific gene or gene sequence that can explain almost every disease and behavioral trait. Through the lens of the Newtonian-Cartesian paradigm, this makes perfect sense. It is highly mechanistic. One particular cause directly results in one particular effect, allowing the complexity of the human condition to be reduced to a set of easily identifiable and predictable factors.

There is much to be said for this theory. There are already a number of diseases where we have identified a direct link between genes and the disorder. In some cases, we have developed very effective (often life-saving) treatments. For other identified genetic disorders, there is promising research under way. Allocating resources to this important work is a no-brainer. Yet, when we begin to suggest that most of our disorders can be cured through or explained by identifying a responsible gene or set of genes, we risk blinding ourselves to the likelihood that there are more complex forces at work that require more dynamic explanations and solutions. There is, as always, room for both.

Fortunately, we are beginning to see some major cracks in the genetic determinism edifice that are allowing room for other theories to emerge. More and more, we are observing the powerful relationship between genes and the environment. The field of epigenetics is revealing that genes by themselves very rarely determine human behavior. Only when we consider them in the context of the environment can we begin to understand why humans behave the way they do. Epigenetics asserts that genes are like light switches. They are turned on, or expressed, in response to some stimulus in their environment. When the environmental stimuli are changed, the theory asserts, so are the genes that are turned on. In one environment, a particular gene will get expressed. In another, it won't. Indeed, there is mounting evidence that the environment is more important than an individual's genetic code in explaining human behavior.[13] The classic nature versus nurture debate will undoubtedly continue to rage. In the meantime, my suggestion is that we replace the "versus" with "and." Nature *and* nurture has a better ring to it, don't you think?

The impact of childhood trauma is a great example of an epigenetic phenomenon. The scientists who conducted the mother rat studies demonstrated that the lack of caregiver attachment causes brains to develop differently. It turns out that the presence of an attuned mother rat acts as an environmental stimulus that turns on, or expresses, the gene responsible for protecting a rat pup from the toxic effects of stress.

Yet the overwhelming evidence of the adverse effects of childhood trauma hasn't translated into a substantive change in public opinion and social policy. Why? People prefer simple theories. Genetic determinism is easier to wrap our heads around. If you have a certain genetic makeup, you are more likely to be depressed, suffer from addiction, engage in violent behavior. Introducing the environment as an additional factor makes things more complex. It's harder to wrap our heads around a theory that requires us to appreciate the interdependency of multiple variables. And, of course, it's much harder to prove and see the cause-and-effect relationship between them. As a result, we continue to allocate resources the way we do, administer justice the same way we have for decades, and fund health care research based on a theory that is insufficient for explaining the complexity of the human condition.

There's another reason many hold on to the theory of genetic determinism: it gives us an easy way out. By attributing the cause of our behavior to our genes, we get to avoid responsibility and the attendant guilt from not taking control of our lives. Nowhere is blind faith in genetic determinism more dangerous than in the domain of addiction.[14] For years, people have tried to understand and explain addiction as an inheritable trait. Early research suggested direct links between genes and addictions like alcoholism. But recent research is at last beginning to shatter this myth. The emerging paradigm acknowledges that genes do, in fact, play some role in addiction. There is certainly evidence that some genes *predispose* individuals to engage in addictive behavior. But, not surprisingly, there is a more important epigenetic component involved.

In one famous early study, rats were placed in an environment where they were allowed to roam freely and were surrounded by other rats.[15] At one end of the rat farm were two water bottles. One contained water; the other contained water laced with cocaine. Rats in *this environment* showed no propensity to drink from the cocaine-laced water despite the supposed highly addictive nature of the drug. Researchers then placed a rat alone in a farm with less space to roam. In an environment with no opportunity for social interaction and less freedom of movement, a rat in the second farm was highly likely to become addicted to the cocaine water. The researchers hypothesized that it was not a genetic trait or the claimed addictive property of the cocaine that caused the lonely rats to become addicted. Rather, it was the stress and social anxiety of the environment that was responsible for the addicted behavior. More specifically, it was the environment that epigenetically triggered, or turned on, the genetic propensity for addiction.

Taken together, this line of research and our knowledge of the effects of childhood trauma have produced a new paradigm in the understanding of addiction. There is now more and more reason to believe that childhood trauma plays a major role in adult addiction. This new paradigm asserts that adverse childhood experiences cause trauma that doesn't simply go away over time. The trauma is literally stored in the body, and it reasserts itself constantly as the brain interprets the near future by referencing the past. An adult who experienced trauma as a child without the loving attunement of a caregiver is very likely going to experience the world as a dark and dangerous place. The resulting suffering and anxiety have to be dealt with. For many, the way to numb the pain is through substance abuse. To make matters worse, research now shows that the very experience of childhood stress and trauma changes the pleasure-seeking parts of the brain, making a person even more susceptible to substance and behavioral addictions. Talk about a bum deal.

Is there hope for those who experienced childhood trauma and didn't have the advantage of an attuned caregiver? I strongly believe the answer is yes. Early childhood trauma has a significant effect on development because of the growing brain's remarkable tendency to alter its structure in response to its environment. Fortunately, the brain retains its ability to change after childhood. This neuroplasticity persists well into the adult years. The pace at which the adult brain can change is slower, but it can change nevertheless. What this suggests is that the effects of trauma are reversible. And if we can ameliorate the effects of trauma, we have a path toward rehabilitating those who have been cast off from a society that is all too often willing to sacrifice its least fortunate members on the altar of the Newtonian-Cartesian paradigm.

I believe we underestimate the power and resilience of the human spirit. I believe that anyone, no matter how severe his circumstances, can be the master of his code. If you find yourself relating to one of the statistics above, I invite you to declare yourself right now, at this very moment, an early master. Committed to powerfully shaping your future. Choosing to be in control and to do everything in your power to shed the imprisoning layers of conditioning in which you are confined. The road ahead for you, as for anyone reading this book, will not be easy. Nothing worthwhile ever is. But if you're committed to leading an extraordinary life, it will be the most rewarding journey you can imagine.

Chapter Four

I Am 100 Percent Responsible for My Life

If you blame someone else, there is no end to the blame.
Therefore the master fulfills her own obligations and corrects
her own mistakes. She does what she needs to do
and demands nothing of others.
—Tao Te Ching

As long as you think that the cause of your problem is
"out there"—as long as you think that anyone or anything is
responsible for your suffering—the situation is hopeless. It means
that you are forever in the role of victim . . . Placing the blame or
judgment on someone else leaves you powerless to change your
experience; taking responsibility for your beliefs and judgments
gives you the power to change them.
—Byron Katie

O ne of the more disempowering, insidious parts of your program is the belief that you are powerless to affect your circumstances. That you are at the effect of your environment.

{Rule: ~~You have little control over your circumstances~~}

This belief will cause you to blame others. It will render you powerless to shape your life. It is a great way to keep you safe and psychologically secure, which is the primary goal of your program. But it will massively limit you in the long run. Mastering your code and leading an extraordinary life require that you believe that you are in control, and that you see and take responsibility for your life in every situation without exception.

I'll start with an important exploration of a concept in psychology known as locus of control. You will see how your belief in whether you control your circumstances affects every part of your life. We will then do a deeper dive into parenting and leadership. You will begin to realize how the radical notion of taking 100 percent responsibility has the potential to transform your relationships and effectiveness in everything you do. We'll conclude by reviewing some of the nuances of doing this work. As with any medicine that has powerful curative properties, it is wise to heed the warnings and follow the instructions for proper use.

***

One of the most important beliefs that you hold is your belief in your ability to control and shape your circumstances. In 1966, a psychologist named Julian B. Rotter developed a theory of human behavior that suggests individuals fall somewhere on what he called a "locus of control" spectrum depending on their beliefs about how much they can influence their circumstances. On one end of the spectrum, *internal* locus of control, individuals believe they have the ability to shape and affect their lives. On the other end, *external* locus of control, people believe they have little ability to control circumstances and that events unfold mostly due to chance, fate, or luck. Most individuals are neither at one end nor the other but rather fall somewhere in between. And a person's locus of control may be different depending on the particular dimension of life being considered. Rot-

ter published a twenty-three-item forced-choice ques-
tionnaire to assess individual locus of control that is still
widely used today.[16]

In the half century since the concept's introduction,
there have been hundreds of academic studies looking
at the correlation between locus of control and dimen-
sions such as health (depression, obesity, cancer, diabetes, etc.), lifestyle (exercise, diet, smoking, alcohol con-
sumption, gambling, etc.), leadership, job satisfaction,
consumer behavior, political ideology and voting behavior, and education and learning. The results have been
consistent and overwhelming. Internal locus of control
is highly correlated with positive results in virtually
every dimension studied—so much so that it suggests
that locus of control may be the single variable that most
explains and predicts human effectiveness.

What is clear from all the research is that an internal
locus of control—the simple but potent assumption that
you have the power to affect your circumstances—leads
to a number of qualities commonly referred to as the Big
Five: taking responsibility, persistence, delayed gratification, seeking information, and conviction. Let's discuss each briefly.

First, people with an internal locus of control (Internals) take responsibility for their actions. They are much
less likely to blame others. The first question they usually
ask is, "What might I have done to have caused the outcome?" or "What could I have done differently to cause
a different, more favorable outcome?" As a result, they
tend to learn and get better from their mistakes. In my
experience and in my work with senior leaders, I believe
responsibility is the most important quality associated
with internal locus of control.

Second, because Internals assume their actions

can directly affect outcomes, they tend to persist for much longer than those with an external locus of control (Externals). This quality of persistence, or grit, has been shown to independently drive effectiveness. Angela Duckworth, a University of Pennsylvania professor, is the author of the best-selling 2016 book *Grit* and is widely known for her 2013 TED Talk that went viral (as of the time of this writing it has more than four million views). Duckworth's work describes research showing the connection between grit and success in people as diverse as West Point cadets, spelling bee champions, and high-paid salespeople.

Third, because Internals believe they will be rewarded through persistent effort, they are willing to delay gratification. Like grit, delayed gratification has received a lot of attention as a major driver of effectiveness. In a series of famous studies conducted in the late 1960s and early 1970s by Stanford professor Walter Mischel, children were left alone in a room with a single marshmallow. They were told that if they waited to eat the marshmallow, they would be rewarded fifteen minutes later with another one. Of the six hundred children studied, about one-third were able to hold off long enough to receive the reward. Follow-up longitudinal studies of these same children into their adult years have shown a remarkable correlation between their early ability to delay gratification and later measures of success and well-being such as increased SAT scores, higher rates of college completion, lower rates of divorce, and better measures of health.

Fourth, Internals seek out information. Believing that their actions can shape their circumstances, they see data as critical, even if the data might not be immediately useful. Externals, on the other hand, believing that circumstances are more likely to be affected by luck or fate, are less motivated to seek out information even if it is potentially helpful. Internals are learners. They have a growth mindset. They use failure or setbacks as opportunities for growth rather than reasons to give up.

Finally, Internals possess a high degree of conviction. Convinced they can affect every situation they face, Internals are less likely to be persuaded to change unless presented with information that convinces them that their position isn't accurate. The great leaders who have shaped history were those who had the conviction to challenge the conventional wisdom of their times. If I had to guess, I would bet Galileo, Gandhi, and Churchill were at the internal end of the locus of control spectrum.

These five by-products of internality may help explain the positive results from having an internal locus of control. In his book *Choice or Chance: Understanding Your Locus of Control and Why It Matters,* author Stephen Nowicki describes the findings from dozens of locus of control studies over the past five decades.[17] The aggregate results are truly incredible. I'll share just few of the areas where locus of control seems to have a meaningful impact.

Let's start with education and learning. Numerous studies have shown that internal locus of control is a predictor of academic success. In chapter eight, you'll see how teacher expectations affect student learning. It turns out, however, that negative teacher expectations don't materially affect students who have a high internal locus of control. As Nowicki explains, "Internality appears to provide protection against the negative expectations of teachers in an academic setting. This is consistent with the idea that Internals resist being unduly influenced by others even when those others have high status."[18] Internal locus of control is also associated with higher retention rates in college as well as a host of other measures of academic success.

The positive effects of internality also extend to business. Across a wide number of studies, higher income is strongly correlated with internal locus of control. Leadership teams where the members are all Internals outperform teams of Externals and mixed teams. Numerous studies have shown that leaders who have an internal locus of control outperform those who are more externally oriented, and the financial performance of the companies they lead is greater as well. In a large study of more than five thousand managers from twenty-four nations, internality was correlated with greater job satisfaction and higher levels of well-being across all countries. Finally, Internals are more likely to be open to change within an organization. As Nowicki explains, "Internals generally behave more positively in response to change and cope better with it because they believe they can, in this new and evolving environment, find ways to affect what happens to them."[19]

Internality, not surprisingly, also plays a role in athletics. Internals are more likely to exercise and engage in sports. They also get hurt less often and recover more quickly from sports-related injuries. Studies suggest that Internals are better teammates, as they are less likely to disengage and more likely to focus on the competitive task at hand. And finally, there is preliminary research that suggests that Internals are more likely to experience being in the zone. The psychological term for this is "flow." This concept, first proposed in 1975 and later popularized by psychologist Mihaly Csikszentmihalyi (pronounced Me-High Chick-Sent-Me-High), is the state of being so immersed in an activity that you experience a sensation of time standing still and of using your skills at the highest level.

Social well-being is also affected by locus of control. Internals demonstrate more positive personality traits than Externals. In one study, participants completed both a locus of control scale and a personality test called the Adjective Check List. Internals scored higher on the qualities of achievement, dominance, endurance, and order. Externals, on the other hand, scored higher on succorance (a measure of dependency) and abasement (feeling guilty and belittled). Not surprisingly, research shows a positive correlation between internality and interpersonal attractiveness. Externals experience greater relationship difficulty. Internality is a predictor of marital success—the more internal spouses are, the greater their marital satisfaction.

External locus of control is associated with greater psychological difficulties and mental illness. In one famous longitudinal study at the University of Bristol in England, researchers tracked thousands of children over several decades. They showed that children who experienced social adversity early in life were more likely to develop depression as adults. But there was one group of children who seemed to be immune to the effects of social adversity—you guessed it, the Internals. Subsequent studies have shown a link between externality and depression. There is also a very significant association between externality and risk of suicide. Internals are less likely to suffer from anxiety disorders and less likely to develop post-traumatic stress disorder (PTSD) after a traumatic event.

In addition to being more likely to engage in sports and exercise, having an internal orientation is correlated with other healthy behaviors. Internals are much less likely to smoke. They are more likely to eat a healthy diet and are less likely to be obese. Externals are more likely to suffer from physical diseases such as diabetes, Parkinson's, epilepsy, and asthma. Moreover, Internals are more likely to cope better with problems such as heart disease and high blood pressure, probably because they are more likely to take their medication and engage in postsurgical rehabilitation.

If this all seems hard to believe, you're not alone. However, if you recall the effects of belief on behavior, the results of this research begin to make sense. If you fundamentally believe that you have the ability to affect your situation, the actions that you see as being available to you will be vastly greater than if you believe you have little control over your circumstances. If you are an Internal, you live in a world where your range of actions and behaviors (and your propensity to take action) is far greater than the world in which Externals live. Internals thus have a far greater likelihood of acting and behaving in ways that are effective than Externals do. A half century of research merely confirms this logical conclusion.

Taking 100 Percent Responsibility

Ask a CEO why her company is underperforming and you're likely to hear something about the competition or the fact that her people are not executing. Ask a parent why there seems to be so much discord in the family and you will undoubtedly hear a complaint about the children being disobedient. Ask yourself why your life doesn't seem to be working the way you would like it to and you will come up with countless reasons—most if not all of which have nothing to do with you.

If you're like most people, your tendency to externalize your problems by blaming and seeking to fix others is a manifestation of the deeply ingrained rule in your program that you have little control over your circumstances. Like most parts of your program, there is some element of truth to this. It is understandable why you would thus seek to blame others and your environment for the things that aren't working in your life. Yet, when you look closely, you will see that this part of your program doesn't serve you. It renders you powerless, albeit perhaps momentarily satisfied.

In the Sermon on the Mount, Jesus warned his followers of the dangers of judging others: "Thou hypocrite, first cast out the beam out of thine own eye, and then shalt thou see clearly to cast out the mote out of thy brother's eye." Few of us heed this warning. Instead, your first response is almost always to blame others or circumstances. Doing so allows you to avoid taking responsibility for your own life. It allows you to be right. It allows you to build community by joining others in the act of collective finger-pointing. Blaming and judging others is seductive. It is our favorite pastime. And yet, if you want to master your code and lead an extraordinary life, it's highly ineffective.

When you blame (and try to fix) others, you selfishly avoid responsibility for your own growth, for discovering and healing yourself. You can't begin to influence and lead others until you take on that responsibility. This simple yet profoundly counterintuitive idea—that change in the world begins with change inside you—can be the key to your freedom and fulfillment.

What would it look like to go through your life unattached to whether others change or not, and being deeply committed to your own growth instead? When called upon to lead and influence others, what would it look like if instead of teaching, you truly led by example?

What if you gave up the right to teach until you learned the lesson yourself? And what if you were equally content whether your own learning (and teaching) resulted in others changing or not?

This state of detachment and inward focus is radical. It requires a courageous surrender of the ego and a continuous commitment to your own development. Nowhere is this more challenging than in parenting. When I first became a father, at the age of twenty-nine, I committed to loving my son unconditionally. And I have done my very best to stay true to that commitment. Yet I was also subconsciously committed to my ego. Without fully knowing it, I wanted the best for my son not only for his sake but also for my own. I took pride in his cute looks, his ability to talk at an early age, his affable way of being, his uncanny capacity as an infant to sit through a meal without crying, his early athletic ability. As he entered the school years, I became emotionally invested in his academic progress and his athletic prowess. Sure, a child's doing well in school and in sports is something a parent can and should be proud of. But I noticed that I began to get frustrated (and sometimes angry) when he didn't appear to try hard enough or didn't achieve the success that I "knew" he was capable of.

I began to see this pattern continue as my first child entered middle school and with my younger daughter and son. What happened to my commitment to unconditional love? What could explain my more than occasional embarrassing outbursts of frustration and anger? It was at this point, during my own early development work, that I began to see what had been previously hidden in my subconscious.

Growing up, I was a small kid. I also skipped two grades in elementary school, entering the sixth grade at age nine. Being the youngest in my class combined with my small stature meant that I was way behind my classmates physically. I was a pretty decent athlete, but I just couldn't compete. As a result, I felt incredibly insecure. I wasn't quite the last kid to be picked for a team, but I was close to it. I began to form beliefs to help me compensate for my lack of physicality and the feeling of inadequacy that accompanied it.

> {My Rule: Being smart is the way
> to be liked}

Being smart allowed me to feel socially safe and to be included. What I lacked in physical prowess, I made up for in academic achievement. This survival strategy worked and subconsciously became part of my identity. After graduating from high school, I finally caught up physically with my peers. I took up sports again and became quite good. Sports remain an important part of my life today.

Once I was a parent, though, I began to see how much I had repressed the part of me that really wanted to be an athlete, that wanted to have the feeling of success on the court or on the field. I first thought that I wanted it for my son, but then I understood I also wanted it for me. Every time I thought that my son didn't try hard enough or succeed in the way I defined success, the part of me that hadn't had a chance to express itself in my youth was triggered. I learned that I had repressed this and other unmet needs into the shadow of my psyche. Now I was projecting this unmet need onto my innocent boy. As I became aware of what I was doing, I began to play with the radical idea of truly loving my children for who they are—not who I wanted or needed them to be. At first, this new strategy felt irresponsible. Wasn't it my role to set high expectations for my children? Wouldn't they be deprived if I abandoned my aspirations for them? The more I practiced unconditionally loving my children, the more it became clear to me that I had no right to project my unmet needs onto them. That doing so was selfish and unloving. That true unconditional love meant loving every part of them without qualification. And that my children would only have the opportunity to flourish if I dropped my selfish desire to meet my needs through their accomplishments.

But what about teaching them? Did I not have the obligation to instruct them in what I knew to be right? My children were counting on me for guidance. The real question was whether I was attached to their following the guidance I gave. As soon as I realized that I could offer direction and be OK if they were not interested in it or not yet ready to embrace it, my relationships with my children transformed. No longer was my parenting tainted with the expectations of followership and obedience. I had finally found a way to deliver on my commitment to parent with unconditional love.

I have come to believe that any teaching that a parent might do comes from a commitment to live one's life in accordance with one's values. As a parent, "teaching" the value of hard work can only come from the parent's hard work. Nothing more, nothing less. If I want my children to eat a nutritious diet, then I must commit to and follow through on doing so myself. If I want my children to be polite and respectful, I must treat them and others respectfully. My children are generally polite and respectful not because I have told them that doing so is important, although I have. It's because they see how I treat a homeless person in the subway or a server in a restaurant. And when I'm imperfect, and I am, they see that I am aware of my imperfections and work to do better.

No one has captured the idea of responsible, conscious parenting as well as Shefali Tsabary. In her groundbreaking book *The Conscious Parent,* Tsabary argues that it is the parent, not the child, who is the real student in the relationship:

> By providing us with a way to shed the eggshell of our ego and step into the freedom that living in our truer state of *being* allows, our children facilitate our evolution. We find ourselves exposed to the truly transformative potential of the parenting journey. With the myth that the relationship between parent and child should be unidirectional shattered, the circular potential of this journey comes into view, as we discover that our children contribute to our growth in ways that are perhaps more profound than we can ever contribute to theirs. Although a child appears in a "lesser than" form, susceptible to the whims and dictates of a powerful parent, it's precisely the child's seemingly less-powerful status that has the potential to call forth the greatest transformation in a parent.[20]

She continues with a revolutionary redefinition of the parent-child relationship:

> To parent consciously requires us to undergo personal transformation. In fact, it's my experience that the relationship between parent and child exists for the primary purpose of the *parent's* transformation and only secondarily for the raising of the child.[21]

I have often said parenting is the best leadership training. And so I have taken many of the lessons I've learned as a parent into my work as a leader and with other leaders. I've done so by becoming increasingly aware of a leader's reactive tendency to want to change others first. In fact, so strong is this need that it blinds him to the place where change is needed the most—within himself. When I sit down with a leader, I watch for this tendency. It is almost always present—more in some than others, but always there.

One of the most powerful interventions I can make is simply to point this tendency out. For most leaders, this may be the first time they have confronted this aspect of their program. It is so deeply ingrained, so habitual, that it frequently needs another person to bring it to their consciousness. Once we have shared this awareness, I then offer the leader an invitation to radical responsibility. I explain that this is the idea that a leader can only hope to influence others if she first takes full responsibility for change within herself. In the timeless words of Peter Drucker, "That one can truly manage other people is by no means adequately proven. But one can always manage oneself. Indeed, executives who do not manage themselves for effectiveness cannot possibly expect to manage their associates and subordinates."[22]

And here is perhaps the most important point. Taking responsibility for your own change cannot be conditional upon others making reciprocal change. Let me give you an example. I had begun working with a leader of a technology company who had filed to go public. In our sessions together, he complained that he was frustrated that his team wasn't acting more strategically. This leader (I will call him Rob) wanted coaching on how to shift the thinking on his team from a focus on short-term earnings to a focus on longer-term competitive advantage and growth. I started with a simple question: "Where are *you* focused on short-term earnings?" "I don't think you understand," he replied. "It's my *team* that's not focusing on the long term, not the other way around." "That may be true," I added. "But I'm more interested in you than your team right now. My guess is that there are plenty of places where you are overfocused on the short term to the neglect of the long term." I then invited him into a thought experiment. "Let's first get clear about all the places where you're engaging in the very behavior that you're criticizing your team for," I suggested. "Then perhaps we'll turn to your team."

Despite some initial skepticism, Rob agreed, and he spent the next half hour describing the multiple ways he had been prioritizing short-term performance and neglecting long-term strategy. It was a humbling experience for Rob, but he immediately recognized the logic of the exercise. "I guess I can't expect my team to do something I'm not doing myself," he concluded. Rob agreed to start his next leadership-team meeting with an acknowledgment that he had not been effectively integrating the tension between short-term and long-term focus, and that he would begin to do so more intentionally beginning with the upcoming board meeting. Most importantly, Rob agreed to refrain from asking the same of his team and to trust that the only thing he needed to focus on was his own behavior. Rob began to get feedback from his direct reports that they felt very reassured by his declaration. Over the course of the next several weeks, he began to notice his team taking more risk and challenging one another in meetings when they weren't seeing enough focus on long-term strategy. It was a powerful experience for Rob, and he has since become committed to radical self-referential leadership as a model for his ongoing stewardship of the organization.

How then do you become more responsible in your parenting, in your relationships, in your leadership? It begins with you noticing your own tendency to want to blame and fix others. Then it requires you to experiment with the radical notion of surrendering this tendency and committing to the courageous journey of discovering and taking responsibility for yourself, first and always. In the timeless words of Gandhi:

> Instead of bothering about how the whole world may live in the right manner, we should think how we ourselves may do so . . . If, however, we live in the right manner, we shall feel that others also do the same, or shall discover a way of persuading them to do so.

Important Nuances of Responsibility

Here's the good news. You now know that, with awareness and consciousness, you have the ability to rewrite your program and shift your beliefs—even your most fundamental ones. So it is with your locus of control. Yet, not surprisingly, the belief you have around your ability to shape your circumstances—the belief that has perhaps the most impact on human effectiveness—is one of the most challenging to change. Why?

First, there is an enormous payoff to having an external locus of control. When you believe you have little or no ability to affect your life—when you operate from a *victim* mindset—you get to blame others for your troubles and avoid responsibility. This is perhaps the most seductive payoff there is. In my work with senior leaders, I find that responsibility avoidance is at the source of almost every grievance and every instance of ineffectiveness. In the earlier example, Rob complained that his team was too focused on short-term performance. I saw this as an immediate signal of the universal tendency to avoid responsibility and to give up the power to affect circumstances. I described how I gently turned the spotlight inward and asked Rob to identify all the ways in which he had contributed to short-term focus, the very thing about which he was complaining. By engaging in that exercise, Rob began to shift from a *victim* mindset to a *responsible* mindset, allowing him to see an entirely new set of actions born from a shift in belief—namely, that he (and he alone) had the power to create change, provided that he was willing to give up the right to blame others and accept responsibility for his life and the outcomes he was seeking.

Beyond the seductive payoff of avoiding responsibility, there is a second reason why shifting from a victim mindset to a responsible mindset is so difficult. It has to do with the common mistaken notion that taking responsibility means *blame*. Let me be clear: saying that you are 100 percent responsible for how your life unfolds does not mean blaming yourself. There will always be circumstances that are truly out of your control. The distinction that I want to make clear is that the belief that you are responsible for your life is not an assertion of truth. Rather, the assertion is a stand to take, a line of your code out of which certain actions become available for you that would otherwise not even occur to you. The real question is not whether the belief of responsibility is true. It's whether the belief of responsibility is more effective—does it lead to better results?

In my work with teams and large groups, I illustrate this point by asking everyone to stand up. I have never had an experience where every able-bodied person didn't immediately stand. I then ask the group why they stood. The most common response is because they were asked to. This of course is true. If asked by someone you have entrusted to guide or teach you something, it would be socially impolite or unacceptable to refuse a simple request to stand. Nevertheless, I ask the group if there are other reasons why they stood. Someone eventually will say because she chose to. Of course this is precisely the point. The truth of why we stand is both because we were asked and because we decided to. Both are true. The real question I'm asking is which reason is more empowering. Standing because you decide to is an action born out of a responsible mindset. It implies that one has choice, and in that choice lies power and effectiveness. The belief that you have a choice to do something is always the more effective belief. There are no exceptions.

Let's consider a final example to illustrate the nuances of this distinction. A few years ago I was coaching a senior leadership team at a prominent technology company. The CEO had decided to take a break from coaching for reasons that I won't get into. After several months, it became clear that the CEO's hiatus was adversely affecting my coaching of his direct reports. It went against a key principle of leadership—namely, that a leader must model the behaviors he expects of his team. More importantly, given the CEO's unique role, it was difficult to be as effective as I wanted to be without his direct involvement. I found myself blaming our limited effectiveness on the CEO's reluctance to be coached— which, in part, was undoubtedly true. I even considered ending the engagement. I then noticed that the one thing I wasn't considering was my own responsibility; it was so easy for me to displace blame onto someone else— in this case, the obvious culprit, the CEO. I had caught myself acting out of a victim mindset, rendered powerless to do anything to improve the situation.

So I asked myself what I would do if I were 100 percent responsible for the success of the coaching engagement. The action that became immediately available to me was clear: I would call the CEO and take the stand that his involvement was critical and that without it our work could not be as effective. Note that I was taking responsibility for things within my control. I knew that I could not force the CEO to be involved, and I didn't pretend that his lack of involvement wasn't affecting the situation. But taking a hard and clear stand for him to participate in the coaching was completely within my control. It just had not occurred to me from my victim mindset. From a responsible mindset, I realized I could and had to give up the right to blame our limited effectiveness on him, particularly since I hadn't even begun to exhaust the options that were available to me. I called the CEO and took the stand I had committed to taking. I was neutral in emotion but powerful in my conviction and integrity. The CEO agreed and resumed coaching immediately.

Operating from a responsible mindset does not guarantee positive results. The CEO could have continued to refuse coaching. What it does guarantee is a greater set of actions from which to choose. The greater the set of available actions, the greater the *probability* of being effective.

One final point about internal locus of control and the power of a responsible mindset. Responsibility has its shadow side. There are a couple of critical, natural tensions that arise when we focus on our own responsibility. We will be discussing polarity thinking and the nature of tensions in chapter six. If we overfocus on any one pole within a polarity to the neglect of its opposite, we will experience the downside of the preferred pole.

This is true with respect to responsibility. The overfocus on responsibility to the neglect of its opposite—acceptance that I can't always control my circumstances—can result in self-blame. Furthermore, it can often be exhausting to operate from a responsible mindset. Exhaustion is an early warning sign that you aren't integrating this tension and that you are neglecting a healthy degree of acceptance that life can't be controlled completely. We would all be well advised to heed the words of the Serenity Prayer:

> God, grant me the serenity to accept the things I cannot change,
>
> Courage to change the things I can,
>
> And wisdom to know the difference.

Another key tension that arises has to do with the importance of unconditional responsibility. I often advise leaders that they must begin with their own responsibility before they even think about making others adopt a responsible mindset. I will even go so far as to say that the responsible mindset must be entirely unconditional. Any hint that your taking responsibility depends on another person doing so eviscerates the power of the mindset. This of course gives rise to another tension. The opposite pole of unconditional responsibility is conditional responsibility. If you overfocus on the former to the neglect of the latter, you become a pushover. You neglect your obligation to demand accountability from others.

The key is to find a way to integrate all these tensions. How do you take the stand that there is always something you can do to affect your situation *and* that there are always going to be things that are outside your control? How do you act both from a place of unconditional responsibility *and* from a place of holding others appropriately accountable? The integration of these tensions is what I call "mature responsibility." It requires thinking that is more complex than unconditional responsibility. It requires a deeper awareness and wisdom that come from a commitment to practicing, to making mistakes, and to learning. It requires, of course, taking responsibility for your own development and the belief—whether true or untrue—that you have the capacity for infinite growth regardless of your circumstances.

Chapter Five
I Forgive Unconditionally

The weak can never forgive.
Forgiveness is the attribute of the strong.
—*Mahatma Ghandi*

Your program is designed to keep you safe from others. Of course, at times you will undoubtedly be harmed by the actions of those around you. Your program makes sure that if you are wronged by someone, you are never wronged again by that person.

{Rule: ~~Never forgive and never forget~~}

This is a trap. If you want a life of freedom, of relationships with the people you love, even if they have wronged you, you must choose to let go of the past and forgive unconditionally.

This chapter is different from the first four. I offer no theories or research suggesting why forgiveness is important. The events of my life are the best thing I have to share about the transformative power of forgiveness. It is the story of how I chose to forgive my mother after more than forty years. And it occurred in perhaps the most unlikely of places—Folsom State Prison.

***

First, a little bit of background. In many ways, I struggle to remember much about my childhood. I have a number of theories about why this is. The leading one is that my childhood wasn't terribly stable, and, to survive and stay intact psychologically, I found it necessary to repress the memory of as much of it as I could. I also did not have the benefit of traditional family rituals, like sitting around a dinner table or coming together on the holidays, where family stories are told and retold, thereby cementing memories of childhood that might otherwise be forgotten.

The little that I can recall about my childhood was insanely volatile. My family moved constantly. Until seventh grade, I attended a different school every single year.

{My Rule: Things can change
at any moment}

This peripatetic existence owed much to my father's questionable relationship with the law. He was a self-described "wheeler-dealer." I came to learn that this meant someone who didn't really care too much about what was legal or not, as long as it meant staying out of jail and making enough money to survive. In my dad's case, wheeling and dealing mostly meant buying and selling a lot of stolen goods—fur coats, shoes, LPs and cassette tapes, arcade games. In later years, it meant counterfeiting designer apparel and baseball cards—you name it. We had something stacked in our house for days or weeks at a time, until my father could sell it and turn a small profit. He also, I would later learn, acted as a "heavy" or an "enforcer" when a person wasn't repaying his debts, someone who showed up at your door with a crowbar and a "don't even think about fucking with me" look on his face. That was my dad.

While wheeling and dealing generated enough money to make ends meet, the income stream was far from steady. Some months, there would be plenty of cash in my dad's pocket. Other months, not so much. As a result, we moved a lot. Often we would break a lease and simply leave our apartment or rented house without notice, only to move to another place where the pattern would repeat itself months later. One year it was a decent apartment with a swimming pool, the next an unfurnished, unheated apartment above a liquor store.

{My Rule: Do whatever it takes to make enough money, and never take money for granted}

My father's "vocation," combined with his aggressive, sometimes violent nature, meant that he spent short stints in jail from time to time. The first one of these (at least that I know of) occurred when I was six years old. I was upstairs with my sister and heard a knock on the door. It was the police, who had come to look for (and found) stolen fur coats. Apparently, one of the officers said something to my dad about his Jewish heritage. That's all it took for my dad to erupt into a violent rage. He punched the officer in the face and was hauled off to jail. He was released with a slap on the wrist thanks to the assistance of a famous Indian-Jewish defense attorney, who had built a practice on successfully defending members of the Jewish gangs in London in the 1960s and 1970s.

Shortly after I turned seven, my mother and father announced to my younger sister and me that we were moving from London (where I was born) to Los Angeles.

I later learned that the move was an attempt to escape a worsening situation. Apparently, my father's illicit pursuits were threatening to catch up to him. Nevertheless, a year later we were back in London. And then nine months after the return to London, we moved back to Los Angeles for good. We would "settle" there, and that's where I would spend the rest of my childhood and teenage years.

I was just about to turn nine after our second and final move from London to Los Angeles. While we certainly weren't settled in the traditional sense, I started to feel that my life had begun to have some stability. We moved into an apartment building in the San Fernando Valley, a large, crowded suburban part of northern Los Angeles. It was one of those classic Southern California late 1970s apartments. Walking distance to the 101 Freeway, a swimming pool in the center, two stories, some palm trees scattered around the perimeter. The apartment building was notable for its eclectic residents. People from all different backgrounds and with all different temperaments. Mostly they were struggling to get by. Drug and alcohol use were rampant. The music wars of the late 1970s (rock versus disco) would play out each night as apartments tried to outdo one another for the loudest stereo system and best musical taste. Left at home for most of the day during that summer, like other kids with working parents, I got pulled into a life that, even at nine years old, I knew wasn't good for me.

A group of older kids in the apartment building had formed a gang called the Stallions. Not being part of the Stallions meant you weren't very cool.

```
{My Rule: Do what it takes to be
 included, even if you have to do
    things you know are wrong}
```

So, of course, I decided to join, which required being initiated through a series of dares. One of those dares was to hang-drop from the second-story balcony. Scared of heights and being sort of timid in general, it took me months to finally muster the courage to do it. Unhurt and relatively unfazed, I then moved on to the second rite of passage—shoplifting. I was required to steal an item—any item—from the local 7-Eleven store without being caught. I chose Binaca, an iconic fresh-breath spray that was popular in the 1970s. It was small and easy to conceal. After completing this second dare, I was on my way to being initiated into the Stallions, yet I was wracked with guilt. I remember thinking that I didn't like the person I was becoming.

Shortly after the Binaca heist, I went for a walk with my dad. It was a typical warm summer evening in the San Fernando Valley. I remember turning to my dad and telling him that this place wasn't good for me and that I wanted to move. He didn't ask any questions. If nothing else, my dad had incredible intuition. He would call it street smarts; "intuition" wasn't a word familiar to a man who had dropped out of school at fourteen. To his credit, he acted on that intuition and immediately moved our family to a rented house a few miles away.

{My Rule: Always follow your conscience}

Not surprisingly, the constant upheaval took its toll on my parents' marriage. I was eleven when they came into my room one evening and told me they were getting divorced. I was going to live with my father and my sister with my mother. I took the news in stride; by this time, I had developed an amazing ability to suppress my emotions and to believe that everything was going to be OK—an essential and perfectly tailored survival strategy.

{My Rule: Everything will be OK—there are always others who have it worse than you do}

In this case, it worked like a charm. I fell asleep quickly that night, content that I was going to be with my dad, who I knew would take care of me no matter what.

Things weren't as easy for him. After my parents separated, my father and I moved to a rented house, which would become the site of the infamous gopher incident. For my twelfth birthday party, I invited a number of school friends over to my house. As we were playing in the backyard, one of my friends let out a shriek and pointed to a hole in the lawn out of which a medium-sized gopher was sticking his head. No big deal, right? At most twelve-year-old birthday parties, this would have gone unnoticed and unremembered. My father, however, took it as an opportunity to add some fun to the occasion. He yelled for all the kids to stand back, which they promptly did. At only five feet five inches tall, my father made up for his lack of height with an intense ferocity in his voice and his way of being. When he spoke, people listened. He lifted his shirt, exposing a loaded handgun wedged in the waistband of his pants. He drew the revolver, aimed it at the gopher's protruding head, and fired. To this day, I have no idea whether he actually hit the gopher. It didn't matter. My friends cheered, thinking it was the coolest thing they had ever seen. And I guess I did too. Not many kids had a dad like mine—one who carried a pistol and shot at small animals during parties. Unfortunately, the parents of my friends didn't share our enthusiasm. I would later learn that after that incident, a number of my friends were no longer allowed to come over to my house. Not that it mattered much. My dad had failed to pay any rent at the gopher house, resulting in our eventual eviction. It was only a matter of months, and we were on the move again.

As strong as my dad was, I'm convinced the dissolution of his marriage, the prospect of raising a child as a single father, and the overall sense of financial insecurity finally broke him. I remember him crying and me hugging him to make him feel better.

{My Rule: You have to take care
of yourself—you can't count
on anyone else}

Things finally hit bottom at one of my soccer games. My dad was the coach of our team. I had gotten injured late in this particular game, and the referee came over to see if I was OK. As I was being attended to, I remember looking toward the sideline and seeing my dad punch one of the dads from the other team. Apparently, my dad overheard this man accusing me of faking my injury. That was the way my dad operated: insult my son and I will make you pay for it. My father was promptly banned by the league from ever watching me play soccer again.

{My Rule: Family comes first, always}

Not one to be told what he could or couldn't do, only about a month went by before my dad snuck back onto the field, keeping his distance to avoid being noticed. His plan didn't work. The league commissioner saw him, stopped the game, and, in front of everyone, ejected me from the game and from the league. I don't remember it being a hurtful or embarrassing experience. My survival program was operating in full force. As a father of three children, I now can see how painful that must have been for me.

Where was my mother in all this? Part of me honestly can't remember. What I do know is that she struggled to adapt to her new life as a divorced woman raising a daughter in a new country with a new culture. No doubt as a way to soothe her suffering, she turned to alcohol. I didn't see her much. And when I did, I didn't enjoy it. By now, I was a highly judgmental teenager, trying my best to make sense of my situation. I disapproved of her lifestyle and of the company she kept. I disapproved of the way she parented, constantly comparing the way my father was parenting me—always showering me with praise and subjugating his own needs to mine—to the more distant and seemingly selfish way she seemed to be with me and my sister. Indeed, I don't remember feeling loved or cared for by her at all. One of the most poignant experiences was an argument I had with her when I was sixteen. I was brash and insensitive and immature. I must have said something to trigger her, and she threw me out of her apartment. As I turned to walk down the stairs to leave, she kicked me in the back. It was at that point that I wrote her off, deciding I'd never need her again. Another rule that I subconsciously added to my program.

{My Rule: I don't have a mother and
               don't need one}

The next twenty-five years of my life were lived out of that part of my program. It shaped not only my relationship with my mother but the relationships I had with other people as well.

{My Rule: I don't need others, I can do it all on my own}

Not needing others became my badge of courage and strength. It was the armor I wore to protect myself. With respect to my mother, it meant long periods of being completely estranged, punctuated by brief, unsuccessful attempts to reconcile. The longest and most painful period of estrangement started when I was in my early thirties. My first two children had been born. My mother met my firstborn. She never met either my second or third child. I took pride in the fact that I was raising a family that was different in so many ways from the one in which I was raised. And I had little interest in having my mother be part of my new family. At the time, there was no way I was going to allow her to take any credit for the children I was raising or to get in the way of how I was choosing to raise them.

By this point, my mother's alcohol addiction had expanded to include drugs. Not just using drugs, but selling them as well. I guess it was no real surprise when my sister called to let me know that my mother had been put in jail for conspiracy to traffic heroin. My sister asked if I would be willing to post bail. I immediately said no (I also shouted some expletives that I'm not including in this version of the story). So strong was my resentment and so committed was I to disowning my mother that helping her was simply inconceivable.

{My Rule: Never forgive those who have hurt you}

She simply did not exist for me. She was released from jail a few weeks later, apparently after the court decided she'd played only a minor role in a small local operation. And so began a decade-long period of complete estrangement.

During that time, my mother was diagnosed with a genetic lung disease. She suffered and knew she only had a few years left. Instead of feeling compassion, I resented her lifelong addiction to smoking. I'm ashamed to say that for many years I even held a grudge that she smoked heavily during her pregnancies. Resentment casts a long and dark shadow. In the last few years of her life, my sister would call me about once a year, hysterical that Mom was about to die. Each year, it turned out to be a false alarm. I became comfortable with my numbness and my ability to disregard my sister's prognostications.

One year, the predictable call came from my sister. This time, it felt different. Perhaps something in her tone or my intuition convinced me to take her seriously—so seriously that I decided I needed to break the long period of estrangement and call my mother. Steeling myself, as I had so many times before, I picked up the phone and called the number my sister gave me. A nurse answered. I told her that I was Hilary's son and was calling to speak with her. The nurse told me that my mother had been talking about me quite a bit. She warned me that my mother was very weak and that it would be difficult to hear her. She then handed her the phone. The conversation was short. I told my mother I loved her. Perhaps for the first time I could remember, a part of me actually meant it. We hung up. I learned that evening that my mother took her last breath about an hour after the call. I was the last person she spoke to.

A couple years went by and I didn't really think about

that conversation, about the resentment I was holding, about anything having to do with my mother. This was part of the narrative I had constructed. I had been abandoned by my mother, I repeatedly told myself and others. And I had been raised by a father who gave me more than any child could ever want. I was both proud of and resigned to the fact that this would be the narrative that defined me. In some ways, it made me feel safe, as if nothing or no one could hurt me. My program left no room for forgiveness. But I clung to it, just like an anxious child clings to a blanket as a way of feeling secure.

Little did I know that this safety blanket was about to get torn away from me and replaced with an infinitely more powerful cloak. One that would be constructed from the inside out. Forged through intimate bonds with the bravest of warriors—men who know more than I ever will about what it takes to feel with real courage and authenticity. What kind of people have the capacity to heal others in this way? In my experience, it is usually individuals who themselves have suffered deeply. In America, we have thousands of institutions that house such people. They are called prisons. Of course, countless innocent people and families have suffered at the hands of those who are locked up in our correctional institutions. Any attempt to describe the people in prison must begin with a heartfelt acknowledgment of this fact. And yet this solemn acknowledgment need not blind us to the reality of those inside.

Until just a few years ago, I was among the blind, oblivious to the realities of those who are incarcerated and the system that imprisons them. Despite my parents' brief stints in and out of jail, I felt no need to see or to understand. I was perfectly comfortable holding a relatively conventional view that those inside our prisons

deserved to be there and that our institutions were reasonably well designed to achieve society's objectives of
protecting the innocent and punishing the guilty. I had no
idea, nor did I care to know, that in the United States, we
house more than two million prisoners. And that at more
than three hundred million people, the United States has
5 percent of the world's people, yet 25 percent of the
world's incarcerated population. Nor did I have any idea
why this was the case or what it was like to be incarcerated. I was content to construct my own walls, like
prison walls, that kept me from seeing the harsh realities
of our penal institutions. This was a comfortable, even
willful, blindness.

And then one day, those walls were shattered. I had
been invited to participate in a program with a nonprofit
organization called Inside Circle. They had been working with groups of incarcerated men inside the maximum security section of Folsom State Prison since the
early 2000s. The work had started in response to race
riots that had been plaguing the prison yard. Stabbings
and murders were commonplace. A group of elders, or
"shot callers" as they were known, came together and
decided something needed to be done. They met in the
chapel of C Yard and started a weekly tradition where
men would sit in circle, put aside their differences, and
create a safe space for them to feel and process their
emotions. The hope was that the healing inside the walls
of the chapel would begin to spread out into the yard
and into the cells where the men were kept. Inside Circle was formed by a former Folsom inmate to facilitate
these weekly gatherings. New men could join only if
they were sponsored by an existing member of the group
and after going through a series of initiating rituals to
determine intention and verify their commitment to the

group's norms of confidentiality and authenticity. Over the course of almost two decades, no inmate who has gone through this work and has been released (many are serving life sentences and have no possibility of being paroled) has returned to prison. A 0 percent recidivism rate is unheard-of. Yet it is exactly what is being accomplished through this program.[23]

When I accepted the invitation to go inside Folsom and work with these men, I had no idea what to expect. A part of me thought that I was going inside to help them. I expected to meet men who were broken, damaged, in need of something. What I experienced was exactly the opposite. These men had begun the courageous inner journey of discovering themselves and looking hard at their programs. They had plumbed the depths of their experience. Each man exhibited a level of authenticity that was like nothing I had ever seen. There was no pretense. No ego to protect. In their words, this was a space where they had learned to "drop their armor." What I witnessed was what it is like to be in relationship with someone where there is no mask, no armor. I was there primarily to learn from them, not the other way around. I began to realize that I was perhaps even more imprisoned than they were. What would it look like for me to drop the protective armor of my program? I was about to find out.

Because this was my first time inside and I was a guest of the group, I needed to be vetted and ultimately initiated. I'm not at liberty to share the details of that process, but part of it included an opportunity for me to look at my "poison"—the part of me that had been wounded and had not been healed. I had no idea where to start. At the time, I literally thought I had no problems or issues that really needed to be addressed. So trying to find a place where I had been wounded was an unpracticed exercise for me, to say the least. Little did I know that perhaps the only place I could find my poison was in the chapel in C Yard inside Folsom Prison.

My experience that first day was profound and, in many ways, life changing. Sitting face-to-face with men who embodied authenticity, I had no choice but to look at where and how I was living inauthentically. I had no choice but to slowly drop my armor and allow these men to see me, in ways that I had never been seen before. About midway through the first day, I was sequestered with two men from the inside. These were my "dogs"— the men who would end up sponsoring me and ultimately be responsible for initiating me into the beginning of what I now recognize as my inner journey. Our conversation began by getting to know one another. We shared our life stories. While different, we had much in common: Upbringings that were shaped by our families of origin. Wounds suffered and unseen. Lives lived out of those formative experiences. Things turning out differently not so much as a result of difference of character as by the gift of good fortune or lack thereof. We were men finding our way back to our true essence, each of us at a different stage of the journey.

I was definitely at the beginning of mine, and we all recognized that. So my dogs did what they were supposed to do and began asking me where I was suffering. An hour went by and there was nothing to show for their efforts to help me see myself. Yet they remained patient and gentle with me. Patience is something these men have had years to cultivate. Gentleness is a different story. I marveled at how these men, in these conditions, could make me feel so safe. To this day, being inside Folsom State Prison with these men is the place I have felt most safe and most seen. At some point, the piercing nature of their authenticity was able to penetrate my armor. Somehow, I began to tap into the pain I had experienced (and had long denied) with my mother. Slowly it came out. The grief, the sadness, the regret, the guilt, the remorse. All of it. I began to cry, then sob uncontrollably, so overcome was I. Years of emotion that I had suppressed was now pouring forth. A space had been created by two men—convicted murderers, who had been cast off by society—to allow me to process grief that I had held inside for forty years.

In that moment, I envisioned my mother, who had passed away a couple of years earlier. I spoke to her. I told her about my regrets. I saw her, for the first time ever, as a woman with her own deep regrets. And then I let it all go. The narrative of the son who had been abandoned by his mother was gone. I apologized and forgave her, recognizing in that moment that there was nothing really to forgive. In the letting go of years of resentment, all that remained was love. Love for a woman who had done all she could with what she had. And, to this day, I believe she heard me and smiled. I looked up, tears streaming down my cheeks, and saw in the eyes of these two men pure kindness, acceptance, and, most importantly, understanding. One of them put his hand on my shoulder. "Good work," he said. "Good work." I smiled back. No more words needed to be said.

That act of forgiveness has changed my life. The energy released in letting go of the narrative I had been holding since I was a child was extraordinary. Indeed, acts of forgiveness almost always have this kind of power. In some cases, they can even reshape history. Gandhi publicly forgave the individuals behind successive attempts to kill him before he was ultimately assassinated in 1948.

I was eleven years old when a Turkish man, Mehmet

Ali Agca, attempted to assassinate Pope John Paul II, firing four shots, two of which struck the pope. During his recovery, John Paul publicly forgave the man and asked all Catholics to pray for his would-be assassin. The pope ultimately met Agca in person and successfully advocated for his pardon. Nelson Mandela was imprisoned for twenty-seven years and subjected to torture by the South African government before being freed in 1990. Rather than call for revenge, he famously sought forgiveness and reconciliation.

When I was growing up in London in the 1970s, I remember my family not being able to go shopping around the holidays, as the risk of an IRA bombing was too high. At the time, most people in England and Northern Ireland would have said that the odds of peace in their lifetime were close to zero. Yet, within two decades, peace was achieved, and for many today, peace and stability in the region are almost taken for granted. The events and actors who played a role leading up to the moment in 1994 when peace was established are well-known. Less familiar, however, is one act of forgiveness that arguably planted the seeds for the eventual reconciliation and cessation of violence.

On November 8, 1987, Remembrance Day, the IRA set off a bomb at a memorial ceremony in Enniskillen, Northern Ireland. Eleven people were killed (ten civilians and a police officer), and sixty-three were injured. The bombing was met with a universal outcry of revulsion and condemnation. The band U2, which was performing at a concert in the United States that day, condemned the attack. Lead singer Bono famously shouted, "Fuck the revolution!" in the middle of a song. Among the dead was a twenty-year-old nurse, Marie Wilson, who was with her father. Following the attack, Gordon

Wilson described lying in the rubble holding his dead daughter's hand. Despite the horror of his personal tragedy, Wilson claimed no ill will toward those responsible for the bombing. He later went on to become a member of the Irish senate and wrote a book in the hopes of bringing an end to the violence. Looking back, the bombing at Enniskillen was a definitive turning point in the conflict. But it was one man's almost unthinkable act of forgiveness that may have been most critical in bringing about reconciliation.

***

Forgiveness may be the most challenging yet essential choice you can make. Most of us hold a deep, unquestioned set of beliefs that forgiveness is tantamount to weakness. That it is important that we don't forget. That we must hold others to account for their wrongdoings. These beliefs are deeply ingrained in our culture. Do you remember the rallying cry following 9/11? *Never forget.* It was an effective and appropriate commandment that we forever remember the event and hold a special place in our hearts for the victims of that atrocity. Yet, at some point, these beliefs calcify into our collective programming, leaving little room for forgiveness.

To be clear, I am not suggesting that you forget or simply let people off the hook for their misdeeds. I am suggesting a more conscious examination and choice in your program. What if you were to shift your beliefs and values so they became meaningfully more expansive? So you could hold the belief in both the importance of remembering *and* the necessity of forgiving? In my case, I chose not to forget my upbringing and my mother's role in it. She undoubtedly acted in ways that were hurtful and regrettable. At the same time, I chose to forgive her completely and to love her unequivocally.

As with any choice, the real question is which set of beliefs and values is most effective for you. I have come to see that a belief set that includes total and complete forgiveness is essential. It is simply impossible to live freely and effectively if you are shackled by the past. Not forgiving is a selfish act of omission. It provides you with a convenient narrative that allows you to avoid taking responsibility for your life. Again, feeling blame and resentment toward someone who has wronged you is understandable. But please remember that whether you were truly wronged is irrelevant if your goal is mastering your code and leading an extraordinary life. The real question is whether holding on to the blame and resentment is serving you. The answer is always no.

Chapter Six
I Seek to Understand

You never really understand a person until you consider things from his point of view.
—Atticus Finch (in To Kill a Mockingbird)

As you now know, your program was written primarily to keep you safe and help you to survive. One of the most common survival strategies is the need to be right.

~~{Rule: Be right, all the time}~~

Being right makes you feel psychologically safe. When you're right you can feel more certain about your self-worth, but it leaves little space for understanding and integrating the beliefs, values, and rules of others. It is much simpler to insist on your rightness. Yet life is a relational game. It's impossible to lead an extraordinary life alone. You have to effectively integrate your rules with the programs of others. You have to choose to understand—and not just in the casual, polite sense of the word.

Seeking to truly understand is a bold undertaking. It requires that you rewrite your program in two fundamental ways. The first is to truly listen. You can't understand another human being if you don't listen. I will explain why it is difficult to listen, how you can learn to transform the quality of your listening, and the impact it will have on the results you get. The second is to integrate. We live in an increasingly polarized world. Much of the divisiveness we experience stems from an inability to integrate differences; in fact, human beings are not really programmed to understand one another.

In this chapter, I will give you a new way of thinking. One that will create a breakthrough in how you live your life and how you relate to others. By the end of it, you will have radically reshaped your orientation to understanding and you will see the importance of understanding in every part of your life.

The Power of Truly Listening

Have you ever listened? I mean truly listened? Quieted your mind and surrendered all self-concern and given yourself completely to another person so that he or she is fully heard? If you're really honest, the answer is likely no. Why is this?

There are a number of theories that seek to explain the challenge of truly listening. According to Bob Sullivan and Hugh Thompson, authors of the book *The Plateau Effect*, the adult human brain has the ability to process as many as four hundred spoken words per minute. The average person might speak at a rate of around one hundred words per minute. So, in essence, when you are engaged in conversation, only 25 percent of your brain capacity is required to track a conversation. Guess what happens. Your brain seeks ways to utilize the remaining 75 percent of unused capacity to process other things. In many cases, you begin thinking about how you are going to respond to the person speaking to you before that person is finished. Or you may begin thinking about something completely unrelated. What you don't normally do, however, is dedicate your unused cognitive capacity to listening fully. This may explain why a young child, with a much less developed brain, can listen so intently. It's not that the child is that much more interested in what you are saying, it's that her more limited cognitive capacity is completely consumed by listening to you.

Another theory rests on a somewhat different understanding of the brain. According to this model, the brain's primary strategy is to minimize cognition and utilize its finite neural capacity efficiently. As we saw in chapter two, your brain is a prediction machine. It compares incoming stimuli to past experience and generates probability-based predictions. In this way, it conserves its limited cognitive resources. When you are listening, your brain is taking pieces of information and then generating guesses about what the speaker is saying or intending to say. Deep, empathic listening requires that you intentionally override this dominant, resource-conserving brain strategy. This is difficult to do. And it can explain why you often find yourself distracted, only partially listening to what someone is saying.

There is also the argument that brains have evolved to prioritize attending to stimuli that signal threats to physical safety. Imagine the time of early hunter-gatherers, when being attacked by a wild animal was a real risk. The humans who were constantly alert to the noise of a predator survived. Those who were deeply engaged in conversation, not so much. According to this theory, part of your brain capacity is reserved for scanning the environment for potential risks. Better to hear the approaching predator and risk missing something in conversation than the other way around.

I will add one last theory of my own, and it has to do with your program. In the modern developed world, your chief concern in conversation isn't physical survival.

It's social standing. When you're listening, you're hearing the other person, yes. But perhaps more importantly, you're scanning for cues that your psychological and social well-being aren't threatened. When you're in a conversation, your program's main concern is you, not the other person. Often, you're listening to ensure you're right, not to identify data that might either complement your point of view or suggest that you are wrong.

Regardless of which theory is more accurate, there is something intuitive to each of them. Experience suggests that true, deep listening isn't natural. And yet, most of us don't really practice getting better at it. I believe you can consciously choose to become a much better listener and that being able to listen effectively can be one of the most rewarding skills you can develop.

Let's start with why true, deep listening is worth focusing on. There are two primary benefits. The first has to do with the gift you are giving to the speaker when you listen fully. Ask yourself how often you are listened to in a way that leaves you feeling complete. My guess is that the experience is rare for you. When you are heard in such a way, the experience is magical. The second benefit is more utilitarian in nature. The more effective and complete your listening, the more data you have. The more data you have, the more accurate your decisions. The more accurate your decisions, the more effective you are. Put simply, more effective listening results in deeper relationships and more effective action. Count me in for working on being a better listener.

Yet, as we've seen, listening is hard work. It requires a full surrender of your entire being. The Chinese philosopher Chuang Tzu captured just how difficult this is:

The hearing that is only in the ears is one thing. The hearing of the understanding is another. But the hearing of the spirit is not limited to any one faculty, to the ear, or to the mind. Hence it demands the emptiness of all the faculties. And when the faculties are empty, then the whole being listens. There is then a direct grasp of what is right there before you that can never be heard with the ear or understood with the mind.[24]

The Chinese symbol for "listen" contains a number of elements, including the ear, eye, and heart:

ear ▶   ◀ you
        ◀ eyes
        ◀ undivided
          attention
        ◀ heart

Marshall Rosenberg, in his groundbreaking book *Nonviolent Communication,* points to our tendency to take things personally as the key obstacle to the type of full surrender Chuang Tzu describes. Rosenberg recounts a dialogue between a husband and wife in which the husband complains that the wife never listens. Through the course of the dialogue and Rosenberg's skillful facilitation, it becomes apparent that the wife's first instinct is to interpret the husband's complaint as an indictment of her. Attempting to try to listen and understand her husband, the wife's first question is "Are you feeling unhappy with me?" A perfectly understandable question, and yet one that is still concerned primarily with the wife's needs. Rosenberg gradually coaches the wife to focus on the husband's needs. Eventually, she asks the simple yet transformative question "Are you feeling unhappy because you are needing to be heard?"[25]

The technique of focusing on the speaker's feelings and needs is perhaps the most effective way to give of yourself fully to the other person. Rather than seeing a speaker's language as having anything to do with you, the key is to put aside your needs for the moment and look for the universal human feeling being experienced and the unmet need of the person speaking. As Rosenberg explains, "We begin to feel this bliss when messages previously experienced as critical or blaming begin to be seen for the gifts they are: opportunities to give to people who are in pain."[26]

If full and complete listening is so powerful and yet so difficult to master, how do you begin to practice this art? As you now know, any new skillful behavior almost always begins with awareness of your program. So it is with listening. In my work with business leaders, I offer the following powerful distinction to create an opening for awareness and for more effective listening: Every time you have a conversation, you bring to your listening the beliefs, values, and rules of your program. These rules constrain and distort what you hear so that what actually registers for you is different from the totality of what is said. I call this "default listening." In every situation with every person, you have a default listening for that situation and person. It is embedded in your program. And unless you are aware of that default listening, the rules you bring to a situation will shape and drive your listening in that situation.

Consider the following example: Your default listening for a speaker at a conference might be "I already know." It will follow that you will be listening only for data that confirm your "I already know" listening, and you will avoid or distort the information that you don't know and should know. This phenomenon is part of a larger truism—namely, that you tend to notice and select the data that confirm your existing beliefs. So if you are aware that you have an "I already know" default listening for a particular speaker or subject, you can then choose to try on a different default listening. You might choose the following: "There is always something new I can learn from anyone about any subject." This intentional choice of shifting from a subconscious, unexamined belief to a new, more far-reaching belief has the potential to expand your listening in a way that is meaningfully more effective.

In my work with large groups of business leaders, I may choose to start the day talking about this distinction. It serves two purposes. First, it equips them with a powerful new leadership distinction that, if practiced regularly, can deepen their relationships and greatly expand the data that are available to them. The second purpose is a bit more self-serving. I will often ask leaders to name their default listening for me. This question always brings some levity into the room and allows me to be a bit self-denigrating. Suggesting that they may have a default listening for me like "What does this guy know about our business?" or "Why are we spending time doing this?" always gets a laugh. More seriously, it allows me to invite leaders to make a choice. Do you want to hold a belief that, while perhaps not entirely untrue, will lead to limited listening and engagement? Or do you want to consciously choose a mindset that allows for the possibility of growth and learning? Again, it is not whether the belief you choose is true or not, it's whether it serves you. Questioning your default listening is about becoming aware of the beliefs you bring to your listening and then choosing a belief that best serves you in that situation.

Try this exercise right now. Identify a situation where you think you could benefit from more effective listening. Perhaps it is with your spouse, your child, or a work colleague. What is your default listening for that person? Be honest. It might be something like "I wish he would just get to the point." Think about how that default listening might be impacting you. In this example, you may get easily distracted and frustrated with the person, causing the quality of your listening and your relationship to suffer. Now, choose and experiment with a new default listening. It might be "I appreciate this person and want to give him the gift of my full attention." Then notice what happens when you bring that listening into your conversation. You might be surprised. Truly listening to this person might allow him to get to the point faster after all.

The need for true listening extends beyond the dyadic relationship of one speaker and one listener. It is in group dialogue where the consequences of the lack of true listening are perhaps most acutely felt. If you've ever been frustrated in a team meeting or other group discussion, you will likely have experienced this phenomenon.

No one has done more to explore the dynamics of group dialogue than the physicist David Bohm. So influential was Bohm in the world of theoretical physics that Einstein considered him to be his "intellectual successor." But it was in the domain of thought and consciousness, and specifically how groups tap into a deeper collective intelligence, that Bohm made some of his most important contributions.[27] Expanding upon the principle in quantum physics that the universe is an indivisible whole, Bohm saw thought and intelligence as collective phenomena. Thus, he argued, in order to tap into our most creative thinking, we must do so through a certain type of collective discourse.

Bohm pointed to two principal forms of collective discourse—discussion and dialogue. The word "discussion," Bohm noted, shares its roots with "percussion" and "concussion," where the basic idea is to break things up. In a discussion, Bohm argues, the main point is to win—for your idea to prevail over the ideas of others. Dialogue, as Bohm sees it, has a much different purpose. It is derived from the two Latin words *dia*, which means "through," and *logos*, which means "the word." "Dialogue" suggests a stream of meaning flowing through and between participants. It is only when the conditions for this type of Bohmian dialogue are present that we can fully connect with the collective intelligence of the group. True dialogue allows participants to access a deeper intelligence, one that is universal and transcends the knowledge of the individual participants.

Joseph Jaworski, author of the magnificent book *Synchronicity* and a student of Bohm's, has spent much of his life teaching the art and science of dialogue. I have had the pleasure of getting to know Joseph personally. He is a treasure. My favorite story of his is of a formative event during his time as a student at Baylor University in Waco, Texas. One afternoon in 1953, an historic tornado ripped through the college town, rendering much of it a wasteland. For the next twenty-four hours, Jaworski and a handful of strangers worked in harmony with one another, knowing exactly what was needed without having to say much of anything. This experience, which Jaworski calls "unity consciousness," was a defining moment in his life and set him on a search to discover the conditions that allow groups to access a deeper intelligence. That search led him to David Bohm and the practice of dialogue.

So how does one create the conditions for dialogue to emerge? The most important requirement is that we listen. And to listen, participants must be aware of their programs. For dialogue to occur, participants must be able to surface subconscious and unexamined assumptions. Once that happens, they have to be able to suspend those assumptions. Bohm suggests that participants "neither carry [their assumptions] out nor suppress them." Rather, he explains, "You don't believe them, nor do you disbelieve them; you don't judge them as good or bad. You simply see what they mean—not only your own, but the other people's as well. We are not trying to change anybody's opinion."[28] In essence, Bohm was emphasizing the importance of awareness of our default listening and willingness to suspend our beliefs and assumptions.

> The thing that mostly gets in the way of a dialogue is holding to assumptions or opinions, and defending them. If you are identified personally with an opinion, that would get in the way. And if you are identified collectively with an opinion, that also gets in the way. The main difficulty is that we cannot listen properly to somebody else's opinion because we are resisting it—we don't really hear it.[29]

During a dialogue, a group is able to access greater

collective meaning because, having transcended the need to defend their programs, participants are engaged in true listening.

So far, our discussion of listening has been admittedly somewhat mechanistic, implying the exchange of data and offering strategies for removing obstacles to the efficient and effective collection of such data. This understanding misses a critical aspect of listening—namely, that listening is an inherently intersubjective, relational act. No one does a better job of describing this than the American author Ursula K. Le Guin. In her essay *"Telling Is Listening,"* Le Guin describes with exquisite beauty the intersubjective nature of communication, both in speaking and listening:

> Any two things that oscillate at about the same interval, if they're physically near each other, will gradually tend to lock in and pulse at exactly the same interval. Things are lazy. It takes less energy to pulse cooperatively than to pulse in opposition. Physicists call this beautiful, economical laziness mutual phase locking, or entrainment . . . When you speak a word to a listener, the speaking is an act. And it is a mutual act: the listener's listening enables the speaker's speaking. It is a shared event, intersubjective: the listener and speaker entrain with each other. Both the amoebas are equally responsible, equally physically, immediately involved in sharing bits of themselves.[30]

True listening isn't thus merely a cognitive act, where you become aware of your assumptions and suspend those assumptions to be able to listen more effectively. Rather, it is an energetic state, one that requires your deep presence and attunement to the other person.

As Le Guin explains, "Listening is not a reaction, it is a connection. Listening to a conversation or a story, we don't so much respond as join in—become part of the action."[31]

Now may be a good time to put down the book for a minute and seek out a loved one. You can change the world if you change the way you listen.

Polarity Thinking—The Importance of Integrating Opposites

You can't understand others if you don't listen. Yet listening, even full and complete listening, is not enough by itself. You have to learn to integrate differences. Here's a critical distinction to help you. Often you will be faced with a *problem to be solved* that has one right answer (or two or more independent right answers). As you progress in your education and career, you are faced with many such problems. Do you go to college or straight into the workforce? Which subject should you major in? Do you take the offer from company A or company B? Should you leave this job and start your own business? At work, you face similar types of problems and decisions. Which candidate do you hire? What assignment do you finish first? Do you ask for a raise or don't you? In your personal life, you face the same endless problem-solving requirements around marriage, child raising, friendship, and so on.

But what about when you face a decision that has two or more interdependent, right answers? This is what happens most often when you are in conflict, when the rules of your program are at odds with another's. For example, think about parenting. If you are raising children with someone else, it is likely that you and your partner have different ideas about how to do it. You may be more controlling, and your partner may be more permissive. In this case, you are not facing a problem to be solved. There is no one right answer. Instead, you are dealing with a polarity (or tension) that can be leveraged.[32] There are benefits and wisdom both to being controlling and being permissive. The problem is that your program will have you see all conflicts as problems to be solved. And guess whose answer you think is right? Yours, of course.

Being aware of the distinction between problems to be solved and polarities to be leveraged makes the difference between average performance and extraordinary results. You can't truly master your code if you don't internalize this distinction. Once you do, I guarantee that you will feel as if you are walking through a different world in which natural, healthy tensions abound. What once appeared as a decision between two alternatives requiring either/or thinking now shows up as a tension that can be leveraged through both/and thinking.

At their most basic level, polarities live within us. Try choosing between inhaling and exhaling and you will quickly discover that breathing is a polarity—we have to manage both to survive. Inhaling and exhaling are inseparable. When we learn to share as infants, we encounter the basic polarity of self and other, which is a tension that we continue to integrate in all of our relationships. Activity and rest is an example of a basic, quotidian polarity. We are constantly leveraging the two poles of that tension. When we leverage it well—when we capture the benefits of *both* activity *and* rest and we minimize the downside of an excessive focus on either one—we are healthy and thrive. When we don't, we burn out or we lose vitality.

Beyond the basic tensions, we encounter paradoxes almost everywhere. In the parenting example earlier, try choosing whether to have firm boundaries with your children or be more lenient. You will soon discover that either/or thinking doesn't serve you well. Armed with the distinction between problems to be solved and polarities, you may now see the dilemma with your partner as a healthy tension that can be leveraged. How can you and your partner get the benefits of clear boundaries *and* the benefits of giving your child enough freedom and autonomy? In leadership, polarity thinking is essential. It is a mark of developmental maturity to be able to recognize and be comfortable with paradox—that there are multiple right, interdependent answers—and a sign that a leader is capable of dealing with and making sense of increasing complexity. I see tensions in organizations all the time. Should you be focused on short-term earnings or long-term strategy? Do you prioritize the team you lead or the leadership team you're part of? In feedback conversations, should you be kind or be direct? Are you focused on your mission or on the bottom line? In making decisions, should you be deliberate (safe) or decisive (take risk)? You can quickly see that replacing the *or* with *and*—in other words, seeing these dilemmas not as problems to be solved but polarities to be leveraged— changes everything and opens up new possibilities for action and effectiveness.

When I was CEO of an organization serving adult learners, we were faced with a classic problem: Do we put our limited resources on our marketing and admissions efforts *or* do we focus on enhancing the quality of our product? About half of my leadership team argued vehemently for the former. We have a business to run, they sensibly claimed, and we won't have a business if we don't have customers. I, as well as the other half of my team, saw it the other way. If we focus on enhancing the experience of the student, which is the right thing to do, we will create a virtuous cycle where satisfied customers become our best marketing engine and drive new student admissions. Makes sense, right? Of course. Both answers make sense. Both are right. And they are interdependent, meaning we couldn't afford to do one without the other. We were trapped in a classic tension and didn't even realize it. As a result, we never really resolved the issue. We tried to do a bit of both and sometimes swung back and forth between the two. The results were subpar for sure, and no one was really happy. Lacking the distinction, I had argued for one pole of a tension without seeing the possibility of getting the upsides of both. What a lesson.

So what do you do when you encounter a polarity? How do you actually leverage a tension? The initial step, of course, is awareness. You have to be able to see the polarity in the first place. This takes a bit of practice, but the awareness of the distinction literally changes the landscape. What you once mistakenly saw as problems to be solved now automatically appear as opportunities to be leveraged.

The second step is to acknowledge that you will always have a preference or bias for one pole over the other. For example, in my leadership I confront the tension of Challenging and Celebrating all the time. I have a preference for Challenging. You could say that I have strong value for Challenging in my program. That's OK, as long as I'm aware of it and acknowledge it.

The third step is to map the polarity.[33] This is where Barry Johnson's pioneering work has been so valuable. In a therapy session with a client in the 1970s, Johnson had one of those famous epiphanies and literally developed, in the session itself, what would become the standard template for mapping polarities. Polarities or paradox was not a new discovery, of course; the wisdom of paradox is a tenet of most ancient traditions. Paradox is at the heart of Taoism, with the yin and the yang symbol speaking to the universal notion that all opposites are part of a greater whole. They are inseparable and give rise to each other. Johnson's genius was to apply this ancient wisdom to the complexity of modern life and to give us tools to be able to effectively manage and leverage the inherent tensions that surround us.

To see how polarities are mapped, let's stick with my example of Challenging and Celebrating. First a bit of background. I was about four months into my second CEO stint, where I had taken over a business that was struggling in an industry that was undergoing massive change. As a result, I worked with my team on coming up with a bold strategy. It required us to rethink almost every part of our business, and it put a lot of pressure on all of us to work hard and perform at extremely high levels. One morning on my drive to a meeting, I received a call from the head of HR, whom I will call Donna. She asked me if I was somewhere I could talk. I pulled into the nearest parking spot and took the call from the car. "I have something that's not easy to tell you," Donna said. "You're overwhelming the team. People love you and respect what you're doing. But they can't keep up. I'm afraid they're burning out and that you're going to lose people." I was stunned. Of course I appreciated Donna's directness and courage, but her words were a direct shot to my ego. I felt unappreciated and misunderstood. And, if I'm honest, angry. My first thought was if you can't take the heat, get out of the kitchen. It took me a few breaths to regain my composure and get curious. What was it that I was doing that was causing this reaction? In retrospect, it was clear: my team was experiencing the downside of my preference for the Challenging pole and my neglect for the Celebrating pole.

Unfortunately, I didn't have Johnson's work on polarity mapping and the distinction of polarity thinking available to me at the time to help me understand and resolve the situation. Since then, I have worked through this polarity and taken steps toward leveraging the tension. It's still a work in progress (and likely always will be), but here's what my polarity map looked like when I was finally able to create it:

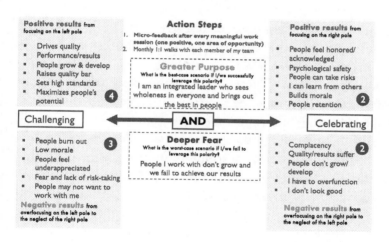

Polarity Map

Positive results from focusing on the left pole	Action Steps	Positive results from focusing on the right pole
■ Drives quality ■ Performance/results ■ People grow & develop ■ Raises quality bar ■ Sets high standards ■ Maximizes people's potential **4**	1. Micro-feedback after every meaningful work session (one positive, one area of opportunity) 2. Monthly 1:1 walks with each member of my team **Greater Purpose** What is the best-case scenario if I/we successfully leverage this polarity? I am an integrated leader who sees wholeness in everyone and brings out the best in people	■ People feel honored/acknowledged ■ Psychological safety ■ People can take risks ■ I can learn from others ■ Builds morale ■ People retention **2**

Challenging ◀━━━━ **AND** ━━━━▶ **Celebrating**

| ■ People burn out **3**
■ Low morale
■ People feel underappreciated
■ Fear and lack of risk-taking
■ People may not want to work with me

Negative results from overfocusing on the left pole to the neglect of the right pole | **Deeper Fear**
What is the worst-case scenario if I/we fail to leverage this polarity?
People I work with don't grow and we fail to achieve our results | ■ Complacency **2**
■ Quality/results suffer
■ People don't grow/develop
■ I have to overfunction
■ I don't look good

Negative results from overfocusing on the right pole to the neglect of the left pole |

Note: Bolded action step is a high-leverage experiment designed to capture or sustain positive results from both poles; circled numbers represent current-state assessment (1 = Never, 2 = Seldom, 3 = Sometimes, 4 = Most of the time, 5 = Always)

In this map, I started by naming the polarity. It's important that you get the tension identified and that both poles are at a minimum neutral, if not positive. For example, Lazy and Energetic is not a tension; Lazy is not neutral or positive. Relaxed and Energetic, or Composed and Energetic, however, would work. Make sure the words you choose have resonance for you.

I then got honest and clear about my preference for Challenging. I listed all of the benefits of focusing on Challenging in the top left quadrant of the map. Next, I moved to the bottom right quadrant and asked myself what I feared if I were to focus on Celebrating to the neglect of Challenging. Immediately, I came up with things like complacency and mediocrity. At this stage of mapping, it usually becomes clear why someone prefers a particular pole. If I fear mediocrity and complacency, then I will naturally lean toward the other pole to avoid that outcome. I then took a hard look at the downsides of overfocusing on Challenging to the neglect of Celebrating and listed these as negative results in the bottom left quadrant. Finally, I identified a number of benefits of focusing on Celebrating. Once I had completed the four quadrants, I did a quick current-state assessment of where I spent most of my time, representing the results for each quadrant in a circled number between one and five. Not surprisingly, I was almost always focused on Challenging myself and others, holding people to high standards, and trying to avoid the fears I had about overfocusing on Celebrating. And I spent little time Celebrating, even though intellectually I recognized the benefits. In other words, I was not effectively leveraging the tension.

I then asked myself, "What's at stake?" Leveraging a polarity and changing behavior is a lot of work. There have to be real consequences if I fail to leverage the tension and a real upside if I do. The downside and upside of leveraging the polarity are listed as my Deeper Fear and Greater Purpose. I came to realize that if I were to leverage this polarity effectively I could become a truly integrated leader who sees the wholeness in everyone and brings out the best in the people he works with and leads. Now *that* was an outcome I could get excited about.

This is where I found the energy to do the hard work of committing to real action items that would effectively get the benefits of both poles. This is about going beyond a theoretical, intellectual exercise and actually committing to new, more effective behaviors. One action I identified that has become an ongoing practice for me is micro-feedback. I no longer wait to give feedback; I give it regularly. And I do it in a way that gets the benefits of both poles. I try my best to find something in every situation to celebrate about the person I'm speaking to. *And* I find an opportunity to give constructive comments where I believe he or she can do better—not because I want to be critical, but because I see the potential and wholeness of each person with whom I work.

I have found polarity thinking to be incredibly useful in giving feedback, which is something we all struggle with. I have yet to find a leader who finds giving it (or receiving it) to be easy. The problem, I believe, is when you get caught in either/or thinking about your own role. Should you be direct or be kind? If you're direct, you think you might damage the relationship. If you're kind, you think you might dilute the message. Understandable, but nonsense. This is a classic polarity. Once you see it as such, you can begin to identify ways you can be both kind and direct. Ways you can give honest feedback and not only preserve the relationship but strengthen it.

The other issue with your thinking is about the other person. Typically, you give feedback out of a desire to fix a problem with someone else. For example, suppose you have a work colleague named Steve who is excessively deliberate. In your opinion, he takes way too long to

come to a decision, preferring to engage in almost endless analysis before arriving at a conclusion. The typical
feedback conversation would go something like this:

> Steve, I'd like to give you some tough feedback. The
> problem is you take way too long to make decisions
> and you overprepare. We simply can't get anything
> done on time and we are missing important opportu-
> nities in the marketplace. People are frustrated work-
> ing with you given your slow pace and your need to
> analyze every last detail. For you to be successful
> here, you really need to speed up and take some risk.
> Not every issue needs to be analyzed.

Is this effective? It's not bad. It's direct. It names
the problem and offers a potential solution. But can you
guess what it's missing? It fails to see that Steve, like all
of us, has a preference for a pole (namely, Deliberate)
and neglects the opposite pole (Decisive). This conversation misses the critical fact that almost all developmental feedback conversations are about tensions. By focusing on the bottom left and the upper right quadrants of
the polarity map, which is what the conversation above
does, we see only half of Steve—the downside of his
preference for being Deliberate and the benefits of the
upside of his neglected pole of being Decisive. Here's
what a more effective feedback conversation might look
like utilizing polarity thinking:

> *You:* Steve, I'd love to talk to you about an opportu-
> nity I see for you. My sense is you place a lot of value
> on being Deliberate. I just wanted to let you know
> how much benefit there is to our team and organiza-
> tion from that preference. The quality of your work is
> outstanding. There are times when we have avoided

making some big mistakes because of how thoughtful you are. And everyone on the team feels like you include them and take their opinions into account. My guess is that you may have some real fears if you were to focus too much on being fast and Decisive, is that right?

Steve: That's right. I worry that if I move too quickly, we could make some serious mistakes. That's happened to me in the past. If I'm honest, I also worry that the quality of my work might suffer and that could jeopardize my standing at this company.

You: I get it. And yet, your strong preference for being Deliberate and thoughtful also has some downsides. Often, you are challenged to make decisions quickly, given the demands and pace of the business, and, with your fear of making mistakes, you can spend more time than we have to analyze issues. I see a real opportunity for you to maintain the quality of your work and increase your speed and, in doing so, capture the benefits of being more Decisive. Do you agree?

Steve: I agree completely. It's something I've struggled with for a long time. I really like the way you're putting it, though.

You: Would you be willing to brainstorm together on some actions you can take to leverage this common tension between Deliberate and Decisive? I have a few ideas.

Steve: That sounds great.

Polarity thinking is a game changer. When you see tensions, you begin to see the wholeness of people and situations. And you do so without giving up your values, preferences, and convictions. In the words of Barry Johnson, "When I can see someone, I can love them." Think about the ramifications of this thinking for your own relationships, for your own development, and for the organizations you work with. And then begin to imagine a world, which today is perhaps more divided than ever, in which people increasingly can see and appreciate the inherent complexity of life rather than be unnecessarily divided by and trapped within the narrow thinking of an either/or mindset. Imagine a world where either/or thinking has an important place *and* is supplemented by the power of both/and thinking. That is a world I'd like my children to live in.

Chapter Seven
I Own My Identity

I'm the king of the world.
—*Muhammad Ali*

Your program is designed to reduce risk and make you safe. As a consequence, your life is composed largely of a series of decisions to go with the flow. To follow convention. To rarely, if ever, challenge conventional thinking.

{Rule: ~~Don't question conventional wisdom~~}

True masters have the courage to say what is unpopular. To challenge the status quo. And even to challenge their most deeply held convictions.

I'm going to introduce you to the power of paradigms. You will see how they shape and constrain your actions. You will learn that to master your code requires the ability to see and question existing paradigms and then create new ones. You will discover that the most powerful and limiting paradigm is your identity—your beliefs about yourself. And you will have the opportunity to reconstruct it. Challenging the conventional wisdom about who you are and what you're capable of is perhaps the most transformational practice you can undertake. It is an essential step to leading an extraordinary life.

***

"*E pur si muove*"—And yet it moves. These were the words Galileo Galilei uttered upon his conviction by the Catholic Church for the heretical act of claiming that it was the earth that moved around the sun, not the other way around.

The idea that the earth was at the center of the universe was widely accepted in ancient Greece and was codified in the second century by the mathematician, astronomer, and geographer Ptolemy. It was not until the thirteenth century—a full millennium later—that this notion was truly challenged. Astronomers began to observe that Ptolemy's geocentric model was regularly failing to predict the actual movements of planets and other celestial bodies. For the next three hundred years, scholars desperately tried to defend and refine Ptolemy's model, so strong was the belief in the earth's centrality. It was not until the work of Nicolaus Copernicus in the sixteenth century that the geocentric paradigm was attacked head-on. And it took another century after that for the geocentric paradigm to be fully replaced with the heliocentric model of the universe, which put the sun, not the earth, at the center of our solar system. Specifically, it took the astronomical discoveries of Johannes Kepler and Galileo Galilei, and the scientific brilliance of Isaac Newton, to put the final nail in the coffin of a model that had persisted for more than a millennium.

Worldviews, beliefs, and myths have incredible staying power. The story of Galileo is particularly illustrative and is worth revisiting briefly. In 1610, Galileo published his first book, *The Starry Messenger,* which described his telescopic observations of the phases of Venus and the moons of Jupiter. His findings directly cast doubt on the Ptolemaic model—having moons orbiting other planets was inconsistent with the notion that the earth was at the

center of the universe. The work was immediately crit-
icized by the Catholic Church, which saw the geocentric model—that earth and man are at the center of the
universe—as fundamental to its teachings. Jesuit scholars remained skeptical despite the fact that Galileo was
able to reproduce his observations. Some were outright
hostile to the implications of Galileo's work, famously
refusing even to look into the telescope itself. In his letters to Kepler, Galileo shared his frustrations:

> My dear Kepler, I wish that we might laugh at the
> remarkable stupidity of the common herd. What do
> you have to say about the principal philosophers of
> this academy who are filled with the stubbornness of
> an asp and do not want to look at either the planets,
> the moon or the telescope, even though I have freely
> and deliberately offered them the opportunity a thou-
> sand times? Truly, just as the asp stops its ears, so
> do these philosophers shut their eyes to the light of
> truth.[34]

In 1616, the Catholic Church, through the tribunals
of the Roman Inquisition, decreed that heliocentrism
was heretical and ordered Galileo to refrain from teaching and promoting the ideas of Copernicus. In addition,
the church ordered all books promoting Copernicanism
banned. Notwithstanding the papal decrees, Galileo's
work continued, culminating in the publication of *Dialogue Concerning the Two Chief World Systems, Ptolemaic and Copernican* in 1632. Immensely popular,
the book describes a series of dialogues between three
men—Salviati, a Copernican scientist, Sagredo, an eru-
dite scholar, and Simplicio, an Aristotelian philosopher
and defender of Ptolemy. Not surprisingly, Simplicio is

made to look the fool. (To add insult to injury, the name "Simplicio" has the connotation of "*simpleton*" in Italian.) It didn't take long for the church to see that its positions were being represented through the arguments of the simpleminded Simplicio.

The church had had enough. In 1633, one year after the publication of the *Dialogue*, it ordered Galileo to stand trial. He was convicted of heresy and sentenced to life imprisonment, a sentence that was almost immediately commuted to house arrest, under which he remained until his death in 1642.

As it turns out, heliocentrism wasn't new with Copernicus. It had been proposed in the third century BC by Aristarchus of Samos, a Greek astronomer and mathematician. And yet the geocentric model went unquestioned for thousands of years. Why did it take so long to expose the myth of geocentrism? What accounted for its incredible staying power?

The Power of Paradigm

History is replete with myths, worldviews, and paradigms that powerfully shape human thought and behavior, and that remain unchallenged for centuries. At some point, these paradigms inevitably reach a period of crisis, no longer able to sustain the overwhelming weight of contradictory evidence, at which time they are shattered and replaced with new paradigms that begin new cycles. This notion of the paradigm was brought into our collective discourse by Thomas Kuhn in his seminal book *The Structure of Scientific Revolutions*, first published in 1962. In it he chronicles the structure of a paradigm shift and explains how the paradigm shapes and constrains the set of actions and lines of inquiry that are available to those trapped within it. Actions and inquiries other than

those accepted as consistent with the prevailing paradigm simply can't been seen. The paradigm serves as
the contextual map out of which human beings construct
reality and make sense of their worlds.

Like the story in chapter one of the fish that can't even
see the water in which they are swimming, the nature of
the paradigm is that it is rarely, if ever, visible. Its shaping and constraining effects are thus largely unseen by
those living within it. The paradigm and its constraints
are embedded in your program. The actions you take
largely conform to and perpetuate the paradigms of your
environment, thus giving them incredible staying power.
History confirms this. For example, prior to the fifteenth
century, cartographic beliefs and emotional barriers had
constrained the exploratory imagination of humans for
thousands of years. It took the bravery, and perhaps reck-
lessness, of explorers like Prince Henry the Navigator
and Christopher Columbus to break through these barriers and unleash two centuries of unprecedented exploration and discovery.

Although not formally articulated until the early sev-
enteenth century, the phlogiston theory—that combusti-
ble bodies contain a substance called phlogiston, which
is consumed when matter burns—can be traced back to
the ancient Greek idea of the classical elements of air,
water, earth, and fire. It wasn't until the 1780s that the
phlogiston theory was superseded by Lavoisier's oxygen theory. More recently, we have witnessed the limits
of classical Newtonian physics. At the beginning of the
twentieth century, physicist Lord Kelvin famously pro-
claimed, "There is nothing new to be discovered in physics now. All that remains is more and more precise mea-
surement." Five years later, Albert Einstein published
his paper on special relativity that challenged the set of

rules laid down by Newtonian mechanics, which had been used to describe force and motion for more than two hundred years.

One of my favorite stories that I like to tell, particularly when I am encouraging leaders to notice and question their beliefs, is the story of Roger Bannister, the man famous for breaking the imaginary four-minute-mile barrier. For centuries, runners had been attempting to run the mile in under four minutes. In the 1950s, the quest to break the barrier took on renewed importance, and a number of famous runners publicly and unsuccessfully attempted the feat. Many of the newspapers of the day began to question whether humans would ever be able to run a sub-four-minute mile. Then, in 1954, Bannister broke through the imaginary barrier, running the mile in 3 minutes and 59.4 seconds. An amazing feat for sure. But here's what's really interesting: it was only forty-six days later that another runner broke Bannister's record. The following year two new runners broke the four-minute mark in the same race. Dozens followed, and as of this writing, more than fourteen hundred runners have accomplished the feat, including one runner who ran two miles in less than eight minutes. Nothing material changed with respect to human anatomy, track conditions, weather patterns, running shoes, or the human diet between the start of Bannister's race and the few years that followed. What then explains the sudden and dramatic explosion of athletic achievement? The only thing possible is the constraining power of the myth that man could not run the mile in less than four minutes. What Bannister had done was not just break the four-minute-mile barrier; he shattered the myth that created the barrier in the first place. The paradigm had offered a limited set of actions available for runners to take. With that paradigm no longer in place, a whole new set of actions became available. Runners were literally free to run through that invented boundary.

Imagine, if you will, that a runner came along and ran a sub-three-minute mile. Impossible, right? Yet, all of a sudden, the actions runners would take—that they could now see as even available to take—would shift immediately. Training regimens, diets, running styles would all be examined, reconsidered, and tinkered with. All of this would happen because a new paradigm had replaced an old one that had locked runners into conventional ways of running. Runners would literally now be running in a new world. Kuhn captures this perfectly in writing about scientific revolutions:

> When paradigms change, the world itself changes with them. Led by a new paradigm, scientists adopt new instruments and look in new places. Even more important, during revolutions scientists see new and different things when looking with familiar instruments in places they have looked before. It is rather as if the professional community had been suddenly transported to another planet where familiar objects are seen in a different light and are joined by unfamiliar ones as well. Of course, nothing of quite that sort does occur: there is no geographical transplantation; outside the laboratory everyday affairs usually continue as before. Nevertheless, paradigm changes do cause scientists to see the world of their research-engagement differently. In so far as their only recourse to that world is through what they see and do, we may want to say that after a revolution scientists are responding to a different world.[35]

What does it take for a paradigm to shift, for individuals to be metaphorically transplanted to a new world? According to Kuhn, paradigms only shift when there is a crisis—when the problems with the current paradigm are significant enough that the exploration of alternative paradigms is seen as critical:

> So long as the tools a paradigm supplies continue to prove capable of solving the problems it defines, science moves fastest and penetrates most deeply through confident employment of those tools. The reason is clear. As in manufacture so in science— retooling is an extravagance to be reserved for the occasion that demands it. The significance of crises is the indication they provide that an occasion for retooling has arrived.[36]

I'd like to offer an additional explanation. For me, paradigms shift and myths are shattered only when there is a fish with the wisdom to notice and ask about the water. Someone with enough courage and maturity to question conventions and see the paradigm itself. I believe that the great explorers, inventors, scientists, leaders, and thinkers have each had such qualities. They have intuitively been able to understand the constraining nature of the paradigm and have had the courage to question the particular paradigms and myths of their times.

You have the opportunity and, dare I say, responsibility to cultivate your awareness so that you can see and question the paradigms within your own program and environment. You do not need to be a great thinker to do this, although you may very well be. You can do this as a parent, as a colleague, as a member of a team, as a leader of an organization, in any area of your life.

I had the opportunity to embrace this responsibility in one of my roles as CEO. The organization I had joined was operating in a highly regulatory environment. Compliance was therefore an essential part of our culture. We simply could not afford to make mistakes; doing so could shut down our business. It was sometimes frustrating to adhere to the laws and regulations of our industry, but there were many positive effects of this aspect of our culture. Most importantly, it inspired a strong attention to detail and an accountability to high standards. At the same time, however, there were shadow effects of our emphasis on compliance. One in particular showed up in the area of employee relations. The organization had become so concerned with the risk of employee lawsuits over the years that it was increasingly avoiding having honest employee development conversations. This in turn led to a dearth (and sometimes complete absence) of written communications documenting performance issues. Given the lack of written evidence, managers felt unable to dismiss employees who were underperforming or, in some cases, who had committed grievous errors.

When I joined the organization as CEO, this vicious cycle had been in place for years. Almost immediately, I began to question why we were tolerating underperformance and why we weren't doing a better job having very direct yet kind conversations with members of our team who weren't meeting expectations. Although I didn't know it at the time, I was playing the role of the fish who could see the water. I had enough wisdom and courage and tolerance for risk to challenge the ways things had been done for years.

In my second month in the role, I was preparing to host a one-day meeting with our top one hundred leaders. This would be the first time I was in front of all of our top employees at the same time. I knew I had to say something about this issue. We simply had to raise our level of performance if we were going to stay in business, let alone succeed. The day before the meeting, I called our general counsel, whom I will call Lisa. "Lisa," I said, "I need to know by the end of the day how many employee lawsuits we've had in the last twelve months, how many have gone to trial, how many have settled, and how much we've spent in judgments and settlements from those lawsuits." Lisa called me back within the hour. "Darren, you're not going to believe this," she said. "I went back over the last five years. An average of nine employees sue each year. None have ever gone to trial. The average amount we spend each year in settling these lawsuits is about a hundred thousand dollars, and most of that is covered by our insurance." I couldn't believe it. An organization of more than three thousand employees was being held hostage and suffering through massive underperformance without facing any material financial risk.

The next day, I started my remarks with an inspiring story of how we were going to reinvent our industry and realize our bold mission. I could see that virtually all one hundred people in the room were engaged and on board. And then I paused. I said that there was no way we were going to achieve this vision if we continued to be afraid of having direct conversations with one another and hold one another accountable to high standards of performance. The days of not having those conversations were over, I asserted, as was the unwillingness to terminate employees who were not meeting the clear expectations of their roles (provided we had communicated with them in an ongoing, direct, and honest manner). A few people raised their hands and offered reasons why this wasn't possible. I thanked them for their honesty and courage in speaking up, reassured them I was listening (which I was), and then told them that we had no choice. The decision had been made. The myth that we couldn't have tough conversations and let people go when they weren't performing to clear and reasonable expectations had been shattered. The vicious cycle had been disrupted, and my choice to question the deeply held beliefs of the organization had provided the conditions for a new virtuous cycle—a new paradigm—to emerge.

Your Identity—The Most Important Paradigm

You have an identity. Everyone does. You likely don't recognize it or would struggle to describe it. But it is there, buried deep within your program. Your identity is the aggregation of dozens (if not hundreds) of beliefs about yourself that you have accumulated over the course of your life.

And, like most parts of your program, the beliefs you have about yourself are not particularly empowering. They were designed to keep you safe. To allow you to grow just enough, but not too much. Your identity was constructed in response to your environment. When you were told by a teacher that you weren't that smart, or rejected by a friend group, or stung by a harsh statement from your otherwise well-intended mother or father, you made up a belief about yourself. You then sought out data to validate the belief you had just constructed. A poor result on a math test was confirmation that you're not really a math person. A former friend who teased you was validation for your emerging identity as a shy person who finds it difficult to form friendships. Your father's endless comparisons of you to your older sister were proof that you were never going to be as good as her.

The strongest driver of human behavior is the desire to be consistent with one's identity. You will do everything in your power to act in ways that fit with the subconscious beliefs you have about yourself. Your identity is the primary paradigm that shapes and constrains your actions. Uh oh. Are you starting to see the connection here? If you want extraordinary results in life, you have to take actions that will lead to those results. But the actions that are required for an extraordinary life are most likely *inconsistent* with your current subconscious identity. The good news is that you constructed your original identity. And anything you constructed can be reconstructed, including that identity.

Identity reconstruction is some of the most powerful work that I do with business leaders. It can be strange at first, but it is almost always transformational. The exercise is simple: Ask yourself, if you want to consistently take actions that produce extraordinary results—in your career, your relationships, your health—what would your identity need to be? Once you've found a powerful identity that resonates with you, you must embody it. To do so, you have to say it repeatedly with massive physical and emotional intensity. This is the only way to build the kind of certainty needed for your identity to manifest.

You may have been fortunate to have subconsciously formed an identity that has served you well. In many ways, I benefited from an identity of high self-esteem and self-confidence. My father constantly lavished praise on me. He would repeatedly tell me how great I was and that I could do anything.

```
{My Rule: I will be successful in
        everything I do}
```

This emerging identity—that I would be great at everything I chose to do—massively served me. My actions were a natural manifestation of this identity. Given my upbringing, I could easily have been a terribly insecure, anxious, and frightened child. It was my identity, however, that allowed me to overcome the potential negative effects of my environment. I thought I was the smartest kid in my class. Whether that was true or not, I behaved in ways and achieved results that were consistent with that belief. I thought I was the best soccer player on the field. And despite my lack of raw athleticism and being younger than my classmates, I played as if it were true, making the varsity soccer team my first year of high school, so strong was this identity and so certain was I of its truth. I just didn't know any better.

Perhaps the most outrageous and illustrative example of the power of my identity occurred when I was nineteen years old and a sophomore at UCLA. I began college at the age of seventeen and supported myself financially. This required me to work full-time. I did so for the first two years of college as a copy boy at a small law firm blocks from the UCLA campus. My principal duty was to photocopy cases for the lawyers at the firm. This was 1989, well before it was cost-effective or even technically feasible to access legal information online.

Despite the menial nature of the job, I loved working there. My aspiration was to go to law school, and the job allowed me to get an inside look into life as a lawyer. I would later have a summer internship and an offer to join the firm after I graduated from law school. But for now, I was a kid who worked in the copy room, whose primary responsibility was to master the art of copying the left and right sides of a large legal casebook in rapid succession. With practice, I cut the copying time of a thirty- or forty-page legal case almost in half.

My interest in the law (and perhaps my copying skills) caught the attention of a first-year lawyer. He took an interest in me and became a mentor and good friend. He was a former debater in high school and college, as was I. We had a shared interest in history and politics. And, most of all, he was what I aspired to be: a young, bright, successful lawyer. I finally had a real live role model in my life.

One day, I received a call from my father at work. I stepped out of the copy room and listened to him explain that his counterfeiting had finally caught up to him. The Ralph Lauren Corporation had sued my father, claiming more than a million dollars in damages. They had hired a prominent L.A. law firm and planned to depose my father. More importantly, however, they had just seized the very little money my father had in his bank account. I told him not to worry, that I would call him back with a plan.

```
{My Rule: There's nothing I can't
       figure out how to solve}
```

I was certain that I could figure it out. I now had a mentor and friend who I knew would help me. I walked over to his office and described the situation. This was the first time that I had been completely open about my personal life with anyone who wasn't a close friend. It was an early and important lesson in the value of being vulnerable. To my surprise, my new mentor was deeply moved and inspired by my story. He couldn't believe that I had gotten to where I was in life given where I came from. He assured me that together we would figure something out.

Whether he knew it or not, he was giving me my first lesson in the law. We spent some time researching state case law. It turned out that California exempts an individual from having his assets seized or attached when his income or net worth is lower than a specified amount. Since my dad didn't technically work or have any net assets to speak of, he clearly qualified for an exemption. We began to draft a motion to exempt him from the attachment and to have Ralph Lauren return the meager amount that it had already seized. Since I couldn't afford a lawyer, I decided I would not only draft and file the claim, but that I would represent my father. In federal court!

The only way to explain the audacity of that decision was my identity. I was fearless, supremely confident, and believed in myself with a level of certainty that defied logic. It was this identity that drove me to show up to court, appearing without a law degree in front of a federal magistrate at age nineteen. Needless to say, the judge was both amused and intensely curious when I appeared with my father. My dad was not a normal-looking man, to say the least. He had suffered from an almost fatal case of spinal meningitis when I was two years old, which left him with the left side of his face disfigured, scarred, and partially paralyzed. My father's dark skin, fiercely penetrating eyes, and a gangster-like appearance contrasted sharply with my blond-haired, preppy-dressed, clean-cut collegiate look. We couldn't have been more different. The contrasts didn't end there. At the opposite side of the courtroom sat a group of four men, lawyers from a prominent L.A. firm, dressed in dark suits, crisp white shirts, and bold-colored ties. The whole image was striking and comical. The judge couldn't contain his amusement and chuckled out loud.

He began the proceeding by asking me what I was doing in the courtroom. Without hesitating, I told him that I was there to represent my father, and that it was my legal right to do so. That I had prepared the brief that was in front of him, and that I was confident that the law and the facts demonstrated without a doubt that my father's money had been taken wrongfully. The judge smiled at me, not out of pity, but I believe out of admiration for my chutzpah. He turned to the lawyers representing Ralph Lauren and, with the look of an angry parent, asked them, "So, what do you have to say for yourselves?" Within five minutes after the bumbling response by the professional lawyers, the judge handed down his order. My motion had been granted, and the small sum of money that had been taken from my father was ordered to be returned immediately.

Surprisingly, I left the courtroom not feeling much. Not terribly proud or happy or relieved. Rather, I felt as I always did. It was simply no big deal. I just did the things that had to be done. Such is the power of identity. It is an energy force that takes its holder along for the ride.

To be clear, I had no idea at the time that I had an identity. And I certainly didn't realize anything about the power of self-image. I was completely unaware that I was driven by a set of rules—in this case, a set of beliefs I had about myself. Mostly, these beliefs had served me well. But not always. My identity certainly wasn't consciously constructed and optimized for the results I wanted in life.

Allow me to share an example. For a number of years, I had wanted to write a book. What I hadn't realized was that I had subconsciously suppressed this aspiration under the weight of a number of limiting beliefs about myself. *I'm not ready yet. I need to learn more before I can write. No one will be interested in reading what I write. I don't even know what I would write about.*

{My Rule: I am not an author}

Because of this programming, I identified as someone who was not a writer, and I acted consistently with that identity. Which of course meant that I was thinking for years about writing a book but not actually doing anything about it. Only someone who identifies as an author will write a book. The paradigm of my identity was working against me. Inside me was a book that needed to be written, but it was being choked to death by a set of hidden beliefs and a story that I was subconsciously telling about myself.

As soon as I became aware of this part of my program, it became clear what I needed to do. I needed to create and embody the identity of an author. Not the identity of someone who wants to or is planning to write a book someday, but someone who is already an author. And I needed to declare this identity powerfully. I needed to say it with the conviction of someone who would not accept any other outcome.

I remember when I was writing this book, my wife asked me if I wanted to include a quick blurb about it in the holiday card we were sending to friends and family. Without hesitation, I said yes. I knew the power of my new commitment and identity. I made a choice to rewrite my program, to question my deeply held beliefs, and to choose an identity that served me. The book you are reading now is a result of that choice.

I have spent quite a bit of time (and gone through several iterations) developing my identity. It is as follows:

I am an extraordinary leader, coach, author, husband, father, son, brother, colleague, friend. I command my mind and body to use every ounce of my unlimited potential and infinite capacity to massively and positively impact the lives of others.

I say this every day, multiple times per day. I scream it out loud whenever I can. (I find the car to be the best place for this, despite the weird looks I get.) The commitment to this practice has been life changing for me. The actions I take and the results I get flow naturally from this identity. It is now so ingrained in me physically and emotionally that I have no choice. My desire to behave in a way that is consistent with my identity is too strong to allow for anything else.

Take a look at your own life. I guarantee that your results are a direct product of your identity. And your identity is one of the most underleveraged assets you have. If you want different results in any area of your life, you must consciously choose, embody, and own your identity.

Chapter Eight
I Never Stop Learning and Growing

All men by nature desire to know.
—Aristotle

How many times when you were growing up did you hear that people don't change? Or perhaps you were told that you were a certain way. An introvert, kind, smart, restless, a troublemaker. Or you heard others described in fixed ways.

{Rule: You have limited potential}

Your response to this aspect of your environment is the part of your program that doubts that you and others can fundamentally change who they are. This belief seeps into every aspect of your life. How you think about learning. Your desire to grow. Your belief about your potential. Leading an extraordinary life requires a commitment to constant learning and growth. This is a path that never ends.

In this chapter, I'll question and shatter two fundamental, related myths that are deeply embedded in our collective programming. Together, we'll explore how your beliefs about your learning potential can significantly impact your own growth and your ability to influence and help others. I'll show you that by simply moving from a set of default beliefs in your program to an empowering code, you will become an exceptional learner and achieve the personal growth that is essential to an extraordinary life.

***

By the early fifteenth century, printed books had existed for centuries, but were still rare. The printing technologies of the time were cumbersome, slow, and expensive. In 1439, an enterprising German goldsmith named Johannes Gutenberg developed a new method for printing books using moveable type. The invention turned out to be one of the most influential of the second millennium. With the advent of Gutenberg's method, it was now possible to print books more quickly and inexpensively than before. What began as a single print shop in Mainz, in what is now Germany, grew to more than 270 cities throughout western, central, and eastern Europe by the end of the fifteenth century, with more than 20 million copies printed. The following century saw this number increase almost tenfold to approximately 150 to 200 million copies.

The result was truly revolutionary. It is no coincidence that the Renaissance and the Scientific Revolution blossomed fully in the centuries following Gutenberg's printing press. The press enabled the massive, widespread sharing of information and ideas, democratizing knowledge. No longer was it held exclusively by religious, political, and academic institutions. The very structure of society was altered permanently.

Wisdom and wise people have historically been and continue to be dependent on books. Of course, the written word is no substitute for experience. The wise person must experience life, not just read about it. Or, as the Chinese writer Lin Yutang stated, "The wise man reads both books and life itself." Yet, one without the other—books without life experience, experience without the written word—seems incomplete. Indeed, the power of the written word (not just the capacity to print it) has shaped and continues to shape history in profound ways.

Consider a few noteworthy examples. When Abraham Lincoln first met Harriet Beecher Stowe, author of *Uncle Tom's Cabin*, he apparently greeted her by saying, "So you're the little woman who wrote the book that started this great war." The novel singlehandedly brought the horrors of slavery to the attention of the American public and, in turn, may have been a tipping point leading to the outbreak of civil war. Then there are the more ancient texts like the Bible and the Koran, which have shaped humankind for centuries. The *Bhagavad Gita* was apparently the one book that Gandhi kept with him while he was imprisoned. The story of Arjuna and Krishna, and the importance of dharma, shaped virtually every aspect of Gandhi's personal philosophy and way of living. Without the *Gita*, as it is affectionately known, we very likely would not have had Gandhi.

And of textbooks, perhaps the most influential of all time is *Elements* by Euclid. Published around 300 BC, its thirteen books formed the foundation for mathematics well into the twentieth century. It directly influenced and enabled the scientific discoveries of Copernicus, Kepler, Galileo, and Newton and helped shape the work of philosophers such as Thomas Hobbes and Bertrand Russell, just to name two. Einstein is reported to have said that a copy of *Elements* and a compass were the two items gifted to him in his childhood that had the most impact on his life and work. It is estimated that it is second only to the Bible in terms of the number of editions that have been published since its first printing.

Our understanding of life itself was reshaped with the publication of *On the Origin of Species* in 1859 by Charles Darwin. The book described the unifying theory for all of the life sciences. Just as important, its main contribution—the idea of natural selection—has become an organizing principle that has been applied across multiple domains. It is no surprise that the book was recently voted the most influential academic book ever written—"the supreme demonstration of why academic books matter" and "a book which has changed the way we think about everything."[37]

Some of the most important leaders of our time have recognized the importance of reading. The recent U.S. presidents Barack Obama and George W. Bush were avid readers during their stints in the White House. A 2017 *New York Times* article titled "Obama's Secret to Surviving the White House Years: Books" tells of the importance that reading played in Obama's years in office. The article describes why the president reportedly spent one hour a day reading:

> "At a time when events move so quickly and so much information is transmitted," he said, reading gave him the ability to occasionally "slow down and get perspective" and "the ability to get in somebody else's shoes." These two things, he added, "have been invaluable to me. Whether they've made me a better president I can't say. But what I can say is that they have allowed me to sort of maintain my balance during the course of eight years, because this is a place that comes at you hard and fast and doesn't let up."

Obama's predecessor was an even more avid reader. The *Wall Street Journal* published an op-ed by presidential advisor Karl Rove that was wonderfully surprising to me when I first read it. Titled "Bush Is a Book Lover," the piece recounts how Bush's years in the White House were marked by a friendly competition between the president and Rove as to who would read the most books in any given year. In 2006, their first year of formal competition, Rove ended the year on top—110 books read that year to Bush's 95. Rove playfully notes, "The president lamely insisted he'd lost because he'd been busy as Leader of the Free World."

It's not just political leaders who are book lovers. There are endless examples of business leaders who count themselves as bibliophiles. Famed investor Warren Buffett is said to spend almost 80 percent of his time each day reading. When once asked about the key to success, he replied, "Read five hundred pages like this every day. That's how knowledge works. It builds up, like compound interest. All of you can do it, but I guarantee not many of you will do it."[38] Bill Gates, Microsoft cofounder and one of the world's most prominent philanthropists, credits reading books with his incredibly successful career: "Every book teaches me something new or helps me see things differently. I was lucky to have parents who encouraged me to read. Reading fuels a sense of curiosity about the world, which I think helped drive me forward in my career and in the work that I do now with my foundation."[39] Indeed, of the business leaders whom I have had the privilege to coach and advise, I have found a strong correlation between reading and leadership effectiveness.

Of course, it's not the reading but the learning that is fueled by reading that is so critical. The futurist Alvin

Toffler quoted the psychologist Herbert Gerjuoy as saying, "Tomorrow's illiterate will not be the man who can't read; he will be the man who has not learned how to learn."[40] It's difficult to deny that effectiveness is not somehow correlated with learning. Those who are drawn to learning seem on average to be more successful. So what pulls some individuals toward learning? Perhaps people are just born with that disposition. Or learning may be a learned habit (no pun intended). Children who grow up in households where reading and other forms of learning are fostered tend to be readers and learners themselves. And it must be acknowledged that environment plays a key role. The more economically secure one is, the more cognitive space (and time) one has to learn. The more one learns, the more economically secure, on average, one becomes.

I first began to tackle questions around learning when I took on the role of leading a career education company serving adult learners. What made someone a learner? How could adults who did not see themselves this way learn how to learn, particularly if they had come from disadvantaged situations? I was convinced that the ability to learn wasn't innate, and I had a hunch that anyone could become a learner regardless of circumstance.

These questions were critical to me in my new role for obvious reasons. I believed strongly that the organization I was asked to lead had a fiduciary and moral obligation to teach effectively. Yet I was also acutely aware that many of our students faced significant and very real obstacles to learning. Some of these obstacles were of the very practical kind faced by single parents raising multiple children and working two jobs with very little support and minimal economic stability. Add to that transportation and childcare issues that made it difficult for some of our students even to show up to class, let alone absorb and retain new information.

Faced with this challenge—how to effectively teach disadvantaged students, many of whom didn't see themselves as learners—I did what I usually do. I pored over the research. I started by reading. I tried to learn everything I could about the science of learning and about childhood and adult development. I visited pioneering programs like *Year Up*, an intensive twelve-month apprenticeship for at-risk young adults. I sat in classes at some of the best-performing K–12 charter schools, which were producing learning gains among disadvantaged students that were mind-blowing. Finally, I decided to teach a class; there was simply no better way to understand the challenges of teaching than teaching myself. And there was no better way to validate what I had been reading and observing than to apply these lessons in a classroom setting.

As we discussed in chapter three, the class I decided to teach was called *Success 100*. It was a class that each of our incoming students was required to take. Its objective was to teach our students strategies for academic, career, and personal success. In preparing to teach, I spent time reviewing the standard curriculum, syllabus, and textbook and interviewed each of our instructors who had previously taught the class. While there were certainly aspects of the curriculum and instruction that were good, I decided to make some radical changes to the way I was going to teach it. My decision was based on two fundamental myths that I was eager to shatter. The first had to do with something called scarcity. The second, perhaps unsurprisingly, involved the very beliefs we hold about learning. Let's address each of these in turn.

Are Poor People Less Intelligent?

Although you may be loath to admit it yourself, there has been and continues to be a myth around intelligence that goes something like this: poor people are less intelligent and less capable of learning. If confronted with this myth, you will likely deny it. You will speak about equality of opportunity and cite numerous examples of famous people who have overcome hardship early in life to achieve extraordinary things. Yet, despite your noble protestations, the myth persists. And it is likely buried somewhere in your program. I knew that it was buried in the programs of our teachers and the students they were being asked to teach. I knew it was likely part of my own program. And so I chose to challenge it. As I dug deeper and deeper into the science of learning, I came to appreciate not only the pernicious effects of this myth but that the myth itself was untrue. I came to believe that, like many of the myths and paradigms we have discussed so far, it was a convenient narrative that allows society to avoid the responsibility for addressing and resolving the most difficult issues we face.

There were a couple of studies in particular that caught my attention and that point convincingly to the flaws in the myth that poverty equals lack of intelligence. The first involved a school in New Haven, Connecticut, where researchers began to notice something very peculiar. Of the two sixth-grade classes at the school, one was a full school year behind the other in learning outcomes. The researchers hypothesized that the striking learning discrepancy was the result of noise—the underperforming class was located on the side of the school next to a railroad track, whereas the higher performing class was located on the much quieter opposite side. When the school installed noise pads in the classroom located near the railroad track, the students of both classes began performing at the same level. Subsequent studies have shown that noise can have a dramatic effect on concentration and performance.

In the second study, shoppers at a New Jersey mall were paid to take a problem-solving test that reliably measures fluid intelligence—the capacity to process information and make decisions. One particular question asked participants to imagine having car trouble that requires a three-hundred-dollar service, half of which would be covered by insurance. Participants were asked to describe what they would decide to do—get it fixed or take a chance and hope the car lasts for a while longer. The researchers found no statistically significant difference in intelligence between high-income and low-income participants on this problem-solving task. They then administered the same test with one specific change to the car repair question: they replaced the language "which requires a three-hundred-dollar service" with "which requires an expensive three-thousand-dollar service." This simple change produced dramatically different results. The higher amount triggered the less economically secure participants to worry about how to cover such an expense. The worry in turn consumed some of their available cognitive capacity, resulting in an equivalent thirteen- to fourteen-point lower IQ score. That difference is enough to move a test taker one whole standard deviation lower—for example, from average intelligence to borderline deficient.

What the heck is going on here? Can noise or financial fears trigger drastic declines in learning ability and performance? The answer is a resounding yes. It turns out that the same effects are true for hunger, sleep deprivation, and virtually every form of scarcity. Authors and behavioral economists Sendhil Mullainathan and Eldar Shafir (the researchers behind the New Jersey mall study) explain this phenomenon in their groundbreaking book *Scarcity*:

> The bottom line is clear. Poverty *itself* taxes the mind . . . [It] reduces fluid intelligence and executive control . . . This suggests a major twist in the debate over the cognitive capacity of the poor. We would argue that the poor do have lower *effective* capacity than those who are well off. This is not because they are less capable, but rather because part of their mind is captured by scarcity.[41]

My students were like the ones described in Mullainathan and Shafir's book. What could I do, I began to wonder, to take into account, and perhaps overcome, the very real and significant effects of scarcity?

Is Intelligence Fixed?

The second myth I began to question and ultimately discarded was the notion of fixed intelligence. I came to see that we all have the ability to affect our learning and level of intelligence, but whether or not we will is rooted in the beliefs we hold about ourselves as learners. Again, consider two fascinating areas of research. The first concerned the beliefs that teachers hold about their students' ability to learn. In 1964, a Harvard psychologist named Robert Rosenthal conducted a study with elementary students in a school just south of San Francisco. He told the teachers at the school that the test he was going to administer was a powerful tool from Harvard that could predict with a high degree of accuracy which students had the highest potential for learning. He didn't tell the teachers that, in fact, the test was a standard IQ assessment with no predictive power. The students took the test and were *randomly* assigned to two groups. A smaller group of students were arbitrarily labeled high-potential learners. And the remaining larger group were designated to be of average learning potential. The teachers were shown the designations, but the students were not. A year or so later, the students were tested again. The group of "bloomers," those who were randomly designated as high-learning-potential children, showed meaningfully higher gains in IQ than those who were randomly labeled average-learning-potential students. Rosenthal and others who have studied this research have concluded that teachers' beliefs about their students can meaningfully affect the way they teach their students and thus the way they learn. This intuitively makes sense. As a teacher, if you believe Suzy has high potential and Johnny has low potential, aren't you naturally more likely to put more effort into teaching Suzy and less into teaching Johnny?

The second research finding is not from a single definitive experiment or particularly fascinating study. Rather, it is the cumulative impact of decades of groundbreaking research by Carol Dweck. Dweck, a professor of psychology at Stanford, has spent much of her career researching the connection between belief and performance. In particular, she has pointed to the effects of two learning mindsets—fixed and growth. With a fixed mindset, you believe that your ability and intelligence are fixed and can't be changed even with significant effort. A growth mindset, on the other hand, is the belief that ability and intelligence can be cultivated through effort. In her book *Mindset*, Dweck writes that your view of your own ability to learn can dramatically affect your success:

For thirty years, my research has shown that *the view you adopt for yourself* profoundly affects the way you lead your life. It can determine whether you become the person you want to be and whether you accomplish the things you value. How does this happen? How can a simple belief have the power to transform your psychology and, as a result, your life?[42]

It turns out that the simple intervention of introducing the distinction between fixed and growth mindset can create an awareness that allows students to *choose* to shift beliefs and dramatically improve their learning outcomes.

With these two myths—poverty equals lower intelligence and intelligence is fixed—now shattered, I began to prepare for my first experience teaching. The twenty-one people in my class were typical of our thirteen thousand students in some respects. Most had not succeeded in traditional education. Many had performed poorly in high school, barely meeting the requirements to graduate. Some had attended community college, only to struggle and drop out due to their limited resources and the lack of class availability. Almost all, however, were determined to change their lives, for themselves and, as was often the case, for their families.

One significant difference was that my students, on average, faced more challenging circumstances. The campus where I was teaching was in the heart of San Francisco on the edge of the notoriously crime ridden Tenderloin district. The class was held at night. The location of the campus meant it catered to a student population that was relatively more disadvantaged than our average student body. One of my students was essentially homeless. He would carry his possessions into class in a shopping bag. I would often accompany him on the walk to the train station after class; neither he nor I would necessarily know where he was heading for the night. Another of my students was on parole, having spent a number of years incarcerated for crimes we did not discuss. He had just left a halfway house, and one of his daily chores was figuring out which form of public housing assistance he would turn to for shelter that particular night. It was clear he also suffered from mental illness, describing to me the incessant voices that would speak to him and remind him that he would likely fail, as he had always failed. Not all of the students faced such daunting obstacles. Many displayed a deep desire and aptitude for learning that had been hindered by their own lack of confidence or the circumstances of their lives.

Reminded that my belief about their ability to learn would affect how I would teach and how my students would learn, I adopted a powerful belief that every one of my students was capable of being an extraordinary learner. And that regardless of my lack of direct teaching experience, I was capable of being an extraordinary teacher. Whether either belief was true was irrelevant. The real question was which set of beliefs would better serve me and my students. The answer was obvious.

There were a number of creative and innovative things that I did in teaching this class. Some concerned the curriculum itself. I introduced subjects like mindfulness and took my students down to our cafeteria during class to do a mindful eating exercise. My students were understandably skeptical. The solution was simple: I showed them an Oprah Winfrey interview with Phil Jackson, which profiled Michael Jordan and Kobe Bryant meditating before games. If Michael and Kobe do it, so can you, I argued. That was all they needed.

At the very start of the semester, I had each of them sign a contract that delineated a list of commitments I was asking them to make:

1. I will always expect the most from myself, believe in my own success, and believe that hard work and effort can change my future.

2. I will expect the best of my instructor and I will give constructive and timely feedback when I don't believe I am getting the best.

3. I will make a commitment to attend every class, always be on time, be prepared for every class, turn in assignments in a complete and timely fashion, and avoid leaving class early.

4. I will dress professionally for every class and I will behave in a manner appropriate for a work environment—including speaking professionally, respecting others, and having a positive and enthusiastic attitude.

5. I will support my fellow students and be vested in their individual success, and be available to help and mentor them when needed.

6. I will refrain from using personal electronic devices in the classroom at all times, and will be an active, engaged learner.

7. I will have fun, treat my education seriously, and learn to love learning.

In return, I signed a contract promising to uphold a set of commitments myself:

1. I will always believe in your success.

2. I will hold you to high standards of excellence and expect your best.

3. I will be supportive and understanding of your personal circumstances.

4. I will always be available to help you succeed. For nonemergencies, I will respond to you within 24 hours (in most cases much more quickly). For emergencies, I will be available 24/7.

5. I will dress and behave in a professional manner at all times and will uphold and role-model the standards and environment of a professional workplace.

6. I will arrive to class on time and prepared and I will bring my best to every class.

7. I will treat each of you with respect at all times without exception.

I also emphasized the importance of diet, sleep, and exercise. For one class, we watched a 60 Minutes special titled "Is *Sugar Toxic?*" and then walked to the nearest grocery store to learn how to read food labels. We compared the actual sugar content with the students' own estimates. We can't learn to be learners, I argued, if we're not smart about what we put into our bodies. Realizing that my students' cognitive capacity would be compromised by the eight p.m. class start time, I decided to bring a shopping bag full of fresh fruit to each class. It was clear that being able to snack on fresh fruit made a difference in their learning and my teaching.

Perhaps the most significant thing I did was to introduce Carol Dweck's work. I did this early, for obvious reasons. If I could get my students to see their own mindsets and switch to a more empowering growth mindset, their ability to retain and learn what I was teaching would increase and they would be building an important foundation for their longer-term success. I started by giving each of them a growth mindset assessment.[43] Not surprisingly, most had a fixed mindset, in some cases significantly so. Together, we explored how such a belief had inhibited their learning and would continue to do so, and what would be available to them if they shifted to a growth mindset. We began to infuse the language of growth mindset into every class. By the end of the semester, I was convinced I had a group of adults who now believed in their potential to learn.

I think of my students from time to time. When I do, I'm reminded of the power of belief and the ability of anyone to be a learner. Most importantly, I see learning as a responsibility. What if I had not dived into the science of learning as much as I did? I'm convinced that the lives of my students would be different, that their potential might still be constrained by their self-imposed fixed beliefs. What about the countless other lives I've had the privilege to touch, as a leader, an advisor, a mentor, a parent, a husband, and a friend? And what about the people I've been touched by? Each of us impacts the lives of countless others. Our responsibility is to do it in a way that leaves each person, and the world overall, in a better place. This can only be done by learning and growing. So go forth and read, learn, and grow—all the time.

Chapter Nine
I Am My Word

Your life works to the degree you keep your agreements.
—*Werner Erhard*

Your program is designed to create options. Like emergency exits in case of a fire, your program instructs you to avoid committing whenever possible, so that when things become uncomfortable or inconvenient you can back out.

{Rule: ~~Avoid commitment at all times~~}

The problem is that your life doesn't work without commitment. And one of the most important parts of your code that you must master if you want a life that really works for you is to honor your word.

In this chapter, I'm going to provide you with a powerful new distinction—integrity—for mastering the making and keeping of commitments. Armed with this new distinction, you will be able to commit to others with greater precision and follow-through. You will have a new language to negotiate the making and receiving of requests. I'll then turn to the commitments you make to yourself and provide a simple yet sophisticated process for understanding and overcoming the frustrating obstacles that seem to frequently (if not always) get in the way of achieving the goals you set for yourself. With practice, you will begin to see that your performance in life is a function of the degree to which you honor your word—to yourself and to others. You *are* your word.

***

Growing up as a boy in Southern California in the late seventies and early eighties meant you likely rode a bike. And your self-esteem was likely tied up in the type of bike you had—if you were fortunate enough even to have one. Those were the days where kids dressed up their bikes with color-coordinated pads on the bike's crossbar and gooseneck. Where the kinds of rims, forks, and handlebar grips you had were a sign of status—and, unfortunately, all too often the subject of ridicule. If you had a Mongoose, Diamondback, or Redline, you were cool. Schwinn, Huffy, or other lesser-known or "inferior" brands were what the uncool kids rode. In my case, my dad found (or stole, I'm still not certain) a used bike that had no brand name on it. Its frame was heavier than the aluminum frames of the best bikes. But luckily for me, it had a diamond in the middle of the frame closest to the gooseneck. It was clearly not the same diamond as the iconic Diamondback bikes, but it was a diamond nonetheless. It provided me the opportunity to do what I often did as a kid. I made up a story that my bike was a European version of a Diamondback and that there were very few of those in the United States. Rare and European. Now that was cool.

I've thought about that bike from time to time. About how invested I was in being part of the cool kids' tribe. About the lengths to which I would go to avoid being teased or feeling excluded.

{My Rule: Do everything you can to
        avoid being excluded}

About how easy it was to lie. And I've begun to realize that despite the fact that my bike was heavier, brandless, and missing some of the cooler parts that the other kids used to trick out their bikes, it had integrity. Not the kind of integrity that we usually mean when we use that word, like morality or ethics, but the type of integrity suggested by the following definition: *a state of being complete, whole, unbroken.* While my words lacked integrity, my bike didn't. It had two wheels, rims and tires, pedals, a chain, forks, a frame, handlebars, and a seat. It was complete. And it performed. Or, more accurately, it provided the necessary and sufficient conditions for performance. It was, of course, up to me to ride it in a way that maximized its potential. Unfortunately, I lacked the athleticism and risk-taking orientation to do much more than follow along, skip the big jumps, and pretend like I was a real BMX biker. That's perhaps a story for another time.

For me, my bike is a metaphor for life and, in particular, the role of language in living a meaningful and effective life. Language is what distinguishes humans from other animals. It is how we have recorded and passed on the lessons of our past. It is our primary method of communication. Language allows us to describe our conditions, our feelings, our thoughts with texture, nuance, and fidelity. Not only descriptive, language is also generative. As we discussed in chapter one, language creates our reality. When we declare something, a new reality is created and people can commit to and undertake new actions. The activities of whole nations have shifted in response to language. When JFK *declared* that we would put a man on the moon by the end of the decade, he did not simply describe a goal. Rather, he created a new future for people to live into. And in response to this new reality, people took actions consistent with the realization of that new future—actions they had not been taking and would not have taken without that declaration.

We see language's generative and creative power in our day-to-day experience. When my wife asks me to pick up my son from soccer practice and I say yes, we have declared into existence a new future, and we both take actions consistent with the commitment I made. Similarly, when you observe companies and organizations, you will see that it is language that creates the conditions for people to coordinate and take action. An organization is essentially a network of communications and commitments. And here's the most important point. Any human system—an individual, a family, a company—can only perform to the extent that the commitments that are made within that system have integrity. Much like a bicycle with a flat tire, if commitments are broken or incomplete—that is, if they lack integrity—performance suffers.

Now you may be thinking, "I always keep my commitments, and if I don't it's no big deal." Let's take a look at that thought, because it's common and, I would suggest, untrue and ineffective. On any given day, you make hundreds of commitments. First, you make commitments to yourself: "I'm going to get up early today and go for a run." "I'm going to eat a healthy lunch and avoid snacks." "I'm going to finish that report that I've been meaning to get to for more than a week." And, like most people, you likely fail to honor many of the commitments you make to yourself. Not all the time, and not in an egregious or untruthful way. But mostly in a way that allows you to minimize the significance of not keeping the commitment. "Well, even though I didn't get up for the run, I got more sleep, which I needed." "I only ate one cookie, which is better than what I usually do." "I got some of the report done, and I'll definitely be able to finish it tomorrow."

You also make and break commitments to others all the time. To your spouse, partner, family, work colleagues, friends. Like saying you'll reply to an email by five p.m. but getting to it later that night. Or agreeing to show up to a meeting at ten a.m. and arriving five minutes late. No big deal, right?

Sometimes you are simply loose with your word. You make imprecise commitments or fail to appreciate when you've actually communicated commitment to someone. Consider, for example, a colleague who says, "I think we should take a look at a new product feature," and everyone in the room simply nods his or her head, but they are all thinking, "What a terrible idea." Or your partner sends you a text (knowing you will read it) asking you to pick up some milk from the grocery store on your way home. You don't reply. Have you made a commitment?

When you are imprecise with your commitments and don't follow through on them, your performance and the performance of those with whom you have relationships suffer. You are out of integrity. Again, not in a moral or ethical or *normative* sense, but in a *positive* or objective sense—not honoring commitments is not necessarily a good or bad thing, it will just compromise your potential for performance. It's that simple. And the only proof I have of that assertion is my own experience. When I honor my commitments, my life seems to work better. When I observe others doing the same, I notice the same thing. When I work with organizations that ingrain the importance of honoring commitments into their culture, they seem to outperform their competitors.

Integrity: A Framework for Commitments

So if you think you might benefit from paying closer attention to the commitments you make (I have yet to meet anyone who can't), let's look at how that actually might work. First, before you even think about honoring your commitments, you have to take a look at the way you make them. For the most part, you're likely quite sloppy, with a distinct lack of precision in the language you use. Consider the following exchange. Person A says, "I need the report ASAP." Person B says, "Sure." Is this a commitment? Well, sort of. Person A has made a request and Person B has indicated her acceptance. But there is no precision in either person's language. The conditions of satisfaction—the conditions that must be met to ensure that the person making the request is satisfied—have not been specified. Both Person A and Person B likely have a set of assumptions that have not been made explicit. For example, Person A knows that if he doesn't have the report by the end of the day, it will delay the project. But he has not communicated that to Person B, and yet he is counting on it being delivered "on time." Person B has a lot on her plate. She assumes Person A knows this but doesn't check with him. So she says yes, assuming that tomorrow morning will be acceptable. Person A and Person B go their separate ways and take action according to their own private set of assumptions. When Person B doesn't deliver the report at the end of the day, and Person A is extremely frustrated because he had canceled other plans in order to review the report that evening, performance and relationship suffer.

Consider the same people who are more precise with their language. Person A makes the following request: "Can you deliver the report by email to me by five p.m. this afternoon? I need it by then because I plan to work on it this evening." Person B accepts the request by saying yes. Or perhaps Person B replies with a counteroffer by saying, "I can't deliver it by five p.m., but would six thirty be acceptable?" Person A might agree or might refine his request by saying, "Could you get the first part of the report to me by five, and the rest at six thirty, so that I can at least get started on my review?" If Person B agrees, they now have a precise commitment. The likelihood that a misunderstanding will result in the commitment not being honored is reduced dramatically.

You get precise with your language when you realize that your language matters. That it carries weight. That, in fact, you can see the truth in the assertion that "you are your word." When you begin to make this shift, you will find yourself pausing before making a commitment. You will ask yourself, "Can I really honor this commitment? Can I really give my word?" If the answer is no, you will either say no or propose an alternative. You can tell people who take their word seriously. They don't give it lightly.

So what do I mean by "honoring" your commitments? You may have noticed that I have been using *"honor"* your commitments, not *"keep"* your commitments. It is an important distinction. If you had to keep your word every time you made a commitment, and you took that seriously, you would reserve your commitments for only those times where you were certain you would be able to follow through. How many times have you genuinely made a commitment, only to have some unforeseen event happen that made it difficult or impossible to keep it? Only making commitments when you're sure you can keep them would cause you to be a pretty noncommittal person. So I use the word "honor" to mean that you give your word with precision and with a sincere intention to follow through. But when you can't follow through—not because it's no longer convenient, but because it's truly no longer possible—then you immediately notify the person who is depending on you and you offer to do whatever it takes to repair the damage caused by your failure to keep your commitment.[44]

Take the example of Person A and Person B above. They have had the second, more precise conversation. It's now three forty-five p.m. and Person B's manager sends an urgent email requesting that all of her direct reports meet in the conference room at four to discuss an organizational announcement that will impact their group. Person B immediately grabs a colleague to try to figure out what this urgent meeting is all about. The four o'clock meeting starts and doesn't finish until five thirty, at which time Person B sends the following email to Person A: "I'm so sorry. I'm sure you heard the recent announcement. My manager pulled me into an urgent meeting and it just finished, so I'm delayed in getting you the first part of the report. I'll still be able to deliver it all, but I won't be able to get it to you until seven p.m." Is Person B honoring her commitment? No. Is she a bad person? No. In fact, quite the opposite. She dutifully showed up to an emergency meeting. Emailed Person A immediately after the meeting ended. And is willing to work late to get the report done that evening. This scenario plays out hundreds or thousands of times each day within an organization. Do you think the opportunity for performance within that organization will suffer? Of course it will. It's normal. It's not bad or negligent. It just massively compromises performance.

If Person B had honored her word, it might have looked something like this: Upon hearing of the emergency meeting, Person B (realizing that she would no longer be able to meet her commitment) would have *immediately* sent a message to Person A and explained the situation. She might have offered to send a draft of the first part of the report right away and asked if there was anything else she might be able to do. She might even have called her manager to ascertain whether she was truly needed at the emergency four o'clock meeting or whether she could debrief with one of her colleagues afterward. In either case, Person A would have been on notice and could have modified his plans accordingly. He would have experienced Person B's integrity firsthand, which would have likely increased his trust and deepened their working relationship. And, perhaps most importantly, Person B would have experienced and felt her own integrity—that state of being whole and complete, knowing that she had honored her commitment to another human being and done all she reasonably could in the circumstances. Imagine an organization or a family where this was happening, not every time, but the vast majority of the time. It would likely be functioning and performing at very healthy and high levels.

What I've just described are pretty straightforward examples. But what about the situations that are a little less clear? What happens if someone reasonably expects you to do something, you are aware of that expectation, but you never explicitly committed to fulfilling it? Is that a commitment? I assert that, in the realm of performance, it is. You are aware that another person is depending on you to take some action. If you don't take that action, performance will suffer—both yours and the other person's. This may seem unfair, and perhaps it is.

But remember, we are not talking about morality or ethics or fairness. We are talking about what works in an empirical, positive sense.

Consider the following example. You are a member of a team at work. Another member is responsible for the agenda for the weekly Monday morning meeting. Every Friday morning, that member sends an email requesting that, by five p.m., each member of the team sends a summary of the progress from that week and the key focus areas for the following week. There is a now a reasonable expectation that you deliver this report, you are aware of it, and if you don't follow through performance will likely suffer. Integrity (in the sense that we have been using that word) requires that you treat the request as if you have directly given your word. If you are unable to honor your word, integrity requires that you immediately let the other person know. At that point, you can simply say no, or perhaps you can counteroffer and ask if it would be OK to deliver the report at a later time. At this point, the meeting organizer is on notice and is able to either accept or modify the request, until you arrive at a precise commitment that you are both intending to honor. This may seem shockingly obvious. But I assure you that this is not the way most people behave. And there is a cost to this regular way of behaving that is subtle (and even unnoticeable) at first but significantly erodes the opportunity for performance over the long term.

What about a person who acts in ways that are incompatible with his stated values and beliefs? Is he acting with integrity? Is he honoring his word? This isn't as clear, but I would say there is a lack of integrity when your words don't match your actions. You are no longer whole and complete, and the opportunity for your performance declines as a result. If you declare that you are a person who values kindness and you regularly act in an unkind manner, you have put your reliability into question. How can others count on you if you act in a way that is inconsistent with what you say is important? And if people have trouble relying on you, they will have difficulty trusting you in other areas of your relationships. Without trust, there is little opportunity for effective collaboration and partnership. Performance will decline.

Here's some good news. You are never fully living in integrity. There is simply no way to always honor your word to others and to yourself or to act in a way that is completely congruent with your stated values. As Don Miguel Ruiz says in his wonderful book *The Four Agreements*, the fourth agreement is "Always do your best." We are never finished. All we can do is do our best and recommit over and over again to living in integrity. To treating ourselves with kindness and compassion (but not make excuses) when we falter, and to learn from our mistakes when we inevitably slip up.

So how do you build the muscle of integrity? It begins, not surprisingly, with awareness. You must recognize the beliefs that will get in the way of any new behavior or practice. There is typically some part of your program that will block you from honoring your word. Often it is your survival strategies. You may recall from chapter three that there are three primary types of survival strategies—belonging, distancing, and controlling. It is usually the belonging strategy that gets triggered in the practice of integrity. This practice, specifically the skill of saying no and being clear about your needs, will often conflict with the need to be included, to be liked, or to please. Imagine that your boss asks you to stay late for an important meeting and you have a conflicting personal commitment that is important to you—a date night with your spouse, a parent-teacher conference, watching your son or daughter perform in a school play. Now it may be that your boss's request is truly critical and that you have a real conflict between a new request that will impact your overall professional commitments and your existing commitments in your personal life. In that case, you will be required to make a choice and perhaps honor your word by speaking with your spouse or family, as the case may be, and offering to do whatever it takes to repair the damage caused by your choice to stay late.

Often, if you are truly practicing awareness, you will notice that the real conflict is between your ego and your word. The request from the boss may not, in fact, be critical. Or, at a minimum, you may simply assume it is without really checking. In any case, what becomes critical is your egoic need to please or to not be excluded, which makes it difficult for you to have clear conversations about what is important to you. You may end up not honoring your family commitments in favor of the new request from the boss, damaging your important personal relationships. Then you discharge your anxiety by creating a narrative that is called "my boss is so unreasonable" and you share that narrative with the coworker at the proverbial water cooler who is more than willing to commiserate, given his own anxiety. What a mess.

Imagine a conversation with your boss that has integrity. Where you authentically acknowledge the importance of the request and share without reservation the importance of your existing personal commitment. Where you are able to respectfully say no and offer a third alternative that might be just as acceptable to your boss as her initial request. Where you are aware of your own program and have the courage to confront it. This is what practicing integrity is like. It's not easy. But there is a huge long-term payoff to honoring your word and living a life that is congruent with your deepest values.

Mastering Commitments to Yourself

One final word about integrity. Perhaps the most challenging aspect of honoring your word is honoring your word to yourself. How many times do you make commitments to yourself, only to discover that you have not followed through on them? Are the commitments you make to yourself any less important than the commitments you make to others? Isn't the impact to your integrity—to your opportunity for performance—the same regardless of whether you are committing to yourself or to others? By now, I'm guessing you have concluded that there is no difference. Yet it's likely that you frequently fail to honor these commitments to yourself.

I believe there are two primary reasons why this happens. First, you place less weight on self-commitments. It's much easier to break a commitment to yourself since you are both the person making it and the one relying on it being honored. How convenient. So the first step in being more effective at honoring self-commitments is to treat them the same as giving your word to someone else. If you plan to eat better, don't simply make a resolution to do so. Really think about it. You are giving your word to perhaps the most important person in your life—yourself. Don't do it without full consideration of the consequences of not following through. Modify the commitment if you have to in order to feel confident that you are giving your word with the capacity to honor it. This may feel excessive, but I encourage you to try it. See what impact it has on you. And be kind to yourself as you build this important muscle. Learn to discriminate between a self-commitment too easily given and one that is given after due consideration. And if you stumble, which you will, practice doing what it takes to repair the "damage" that is caused by failing to honor your word to yourself.

The second reason why you might find it challenging to honor your word to yourself has to do with the deeper parts of your program. I have found the work of Bob Kegan, whom you met in chapter one, and his colleague Lisa Lahey, both professors of psychology at Harvard, to be particularly instructive. Kegan and Lahey argue that what lies between a commitment to do something and actually doing it is a subconscious, unexamined "psychological immune system." They have developed a framework called "immunity to change" (I prefer to call it "immunity to commitment") that provides a step-by-step process for disaggregating this immune system.[45] The process contains five steps and can be applied to any commitment you make.

Before reading any further, I invite you to find something to write with and to take a minute or two to identify a commitment that you have made or would like to make to be more effective—either personally or professionally.[46]

The commitment you identify in this first step needs to be something that is really compelling and exciting, something worth subjecting yourself to a deep process of personal exploration. Once you've identified that thing, make sure you write it down and phrase it in the affirmative. Here's what an effective commitment might look like: *I am committed to spending more quality time with my teenage daughter.* This is an affirmative statement of what you are committed to doing to be better at something. Remember, you are your word, so don't make the commitment lightly.

The second step is to write a list of all the things you

are doing and not doing that are inconsistent with the commitment. This list of undermining behaviors doesn't need to be exhaustive, but you shouldn't hold back. A good doing/not doing inventory will most likely contain some embarrassing things. For example: *I often think about work when I'm spending time with my daughter.* Remember, this is a list of things you are *doing* or not *doing*. It is not a list of feeling states. For example, *I become distracted when I'm with my daughter* is not quite the same as *I often think about work when I'm with my daughter.* Focus on specific actions you are doing or not doing.

The third step is actually divided into two parts. The first is to think about the worries and fears that come up when you imagine doing the opposite of each of the undermining behaviors listed in the second step. I find that it is helpful to ask, "What is the worst consequence if I were to do the opposite of this undermining behavior?" For example, if you were to imagine not thinking about work when you're spending time with your daughter, you might discover that you're worried *I will miss the opportunity to come up with a really good idea* or *I will forget about an important call or email that I have to send.* Whatever comes up for you, write it down. The second part of this step is to reframe each of the worries into a hidden commitment. For example, you would reframe your worry *I will forget about an important call or email that I have to send* as follows: *I am committed to not forgetting about important calls or emails.* In this part of the step, you are trying to diagnose misguided forms of self-protection. Often these hidden commitments will seem petty or ridiculous. That's OK and to be expected. Your list of hidden commitments should show that the undermining behaviors you listed in the second step now make perfect sense.

The fourth step requires you to pause, review what you have discovered so far, and ask yourself the following question: What does this information suggest about my big assumptions in life? About how I see myself and how the world works? This is the step where you really begin to look at the deeper parts of your program.

As you examine the first three steps of this process, you will likely begin to uncover that what stands in the way of your commitment to spend more quality time with your daughter may be a deep need for financial security or a belief that your work must come first. Or, at an even deeper level, that the world is an unsafe place. The point of this important step is to begin to identify core, subconscious beliefs that are part of your program. One of the most important steps toward mastering your code is to identify and examine your beliefs and to move from a place of being subject to those beliefs to being able to hold those beliefs as object and exercise some degree of choice over them. This step is the place for that examination.

The fifth and final step in the process is to question the one big assumption from step four that really resonates with you. It might be *I assume that my work will suffer if I'm not always available and open to thinking about it.* The first part of this step is for you to simply *notice and observe*. Where in your life are you making this assumption? What behavior does this assumption result in? What are the consequences? What *evidence can you find that the assumption isn't true*? Perhaps there are plenty of places where you don't focus on work and your work doesn't suffer. You might exercise for an hour or enjoy a date night with your partner without any thought of work and without any of your work suffering. The second part of this step is to *conduct a specific experiment*. An effective experiment is time bound, usually thirty days. It involves practicing a new behavior regularly, ideally daily. And it is low-risk. Your experiment might be that you decide to turn off your phone and computer at a certain time each evening and not check email until you've exercised and had breakfast. You could give your colleagues and clients an alternative way to contact you in case of a genuine business emergency. You could then collect data and learn. What did your experiment tell you about your big assumption? What would it look like if you incorporated what you learned more intentionally into your daily life and personal relationships? And, most importantly, how will they create new possibilities for a more fulfilling relationship with your teenage daughter?

Integrity—the practice of honoring your word—has the potential to massively increase your performance in every dimension of your life. Your relationships, your work, your overall well-being. To master your code, you have to master your word. You must go forth and declare "I *am* my word."

Chapter Ten
I Live on Purpose

Find out who you are, and do it on purpose.
—Dolly Parton

By now I hope you realize that your life is yours to shape. No longer controlled or confined by the rules of your program, you have the ability to create a code and live the life you want. This doesn't mean that circumstances and events won't get in your way. What it means is that you will see them as moveable. You will own your capacity to overcome the obstacles in your path. You will know that the biggest of those obstacles is the meaning you give to your circumstances, not the circumstances themselves.

Yet there is still one final part of your program to contend with. It is the part that speaks to the bigger picture. It is the one that describes the story of your life. What you think you are supposed to do. Your destiny. Your program has likely steered you toward a life that others want for you, that will keep you safe. It does not want you to venture out, to take risks, to see what you're truly capable of, to discover what you're really meant to do in this world.

{Rule: ~~There's little you can do to shape your destiny~~}

In this chapter, I'll argue that you are endowed with a unique calling. You likely don't know this calling exists and what it is. And you probably haven't nurtured it. Having definitively chosen to master your code, your final step is to identify your calling and live it on purpose. I'll lay out the path for doing just that. I encourage you to actively read each of the six steps of this path, as if you are an explorer of your life, trying to discover the hidden treasure that will change everything for you. To fully master your code and lead an extraordinary life requires that you discover and commit to your calling. You must choose to live on purpose.

***

Sometime in the twelfth or thirteenth century, a group of Thai monks commissioned the construction of a gold statue of the Buddha. For five hundred years or so, the statue remained essentially untouched, passing from generation to generation of monks. In 1767, the statue was completely plastered with a thick layer of stucco to conceal it from an invading Burmese army, which was intent on destroying anything of value. Although virtually all of the Thai monks perished in the Burmese attack, the strategy to protect the statue worked. For almost two hundred years after the invasion, the statue remained housed in a temple in Bangkok among other ruins, its true nature and value having been forgotten. Then, in 1955, the statue had to be moved to another section of the temple. During the move, the statue was accidentally dropped, cracking the stucco. Closer inspection revealed that the statue was actually made of gold. The plaster was completely removed and the statue restored to its original state. Today, the Golden Buddha shines in all its original glory, standing at more than ten feet tall, weighing over five tons, and valued at more than $250 million.

I am particularly fond of this story. Like Michelangelo's quote, "I saw the angel in the marble and carved until I set him free," the story serves as a powerful metaphor—that each of us is pure and precious at our core. You came into this world with a gift, a calling. It is at the core of who you are. Yet, as you have gone through life, you likely added layer upon layer of material on top of your core, mostly to protect yourself, much like the Thai monks did to keep the Golden Buddha safe. The protective layers are the rules of your program. Over time, these layers have likely obscured your unique gift or calling.

The last stage in mastering your code is to discover and commit to your calling. But how do you do this? While everyone's path will be unique and won't necessarily follow a straight line, I want to propose a path for the person like you who has chosen to master his or her code and who wants to live life on purpose. There are six essential steps:

1. Discover your calling
2. Overcome resistance and doubt
3. Commit to the path of mastery
4. Let go of the outcome
5. Have faith
6. Embrace your mortality

Step One: Discover Your Calling

The notion of an essential calling is part of almost every religious, philosophical, and spiritual tradition. In Indian philosophy and religion, it is known as dharma.

While there is no one definition of dharma, the meaning given to it by the yogic traditions is for me the most useful. Essentially, it is claimed that each human being has a unique, essential sacred vocation. It is each individual's responsibility to completely embody, nurture, and fulfill this calling. In his wonderful book *The Great Work of Your Life*, author Stephen Cope offers the following definition of dharma: "We might say that every person's dharma is like an internal fingerprint. It is the subtle interior blueprint of a soul."[47]

The Greek philosophers referred to one's essential reason for being as "*entelechy*," which Aristotle defined as "that which turns potential into reality." The Jesuit priest and philosopher Pierre Teilhard de Chardin is reported to have described the term as follows: "It means the dynamic purpose that is coded in you. It is the entelechy of this acorn on the ground to be an oak tree. It is the entelechy of that baby over there to be a grown-up human being. It is the entelechy of the caterpillar to undergo metamorphosis and become a butterfly."[48]

The Japanese have the concept of *ikigai*. It means "reason for living" or "the reason for getting out of bed in the morning." Ikigai is described as the intersection of four things: what I love to do, what the world needs, what I can get paid for, and what I'm good at. Dan Buettner, the author of The *Blue Zones: Lessons for Living Longer from the People Who've Lived the Longest*, argues that people who have a culture of ikigai, like the Okinawans, tend to live longer. He has found the same to be true of other "blue zones"—people who live with and out of a sense of purpose tend to have longer lives.

One of my favorite examples of identifying one's calling is a story from Jane Goodall, the world-renowned primatologist and anthropologist. Goodall recounts that when she was four years old, she was staying at her family's farm. It was her job to collect the hen's eggs. She became fascinated with how a hen could lay something as large as an egg. One morning, she woke up early and, without telling anyone, snuck into the barn. She hid in a place where the hens would not notice her and remained silent and still for hours, so intent was she on understanding the mystery of egg laying. Her family awoke to find the four-year-old Jane missing. Panic ensued, the police were summoned, and a search and rescue mission was assembled. Unaware of the commotion she was causing, Jane remained still. Finally, a hen came into the barn, sat upon her nest, and laid an egg right before the entranced child. Thrilled by her discovery, Jane came running out of the barn toward her mother. Rather than yell at and berate the child, as I'm sure most parents would naturally have done, Jane's mother instinctively noticed something about her. As Jane tells it, "Despite her worry, when mum, still searching, saw the excited little girl rushing toward the house, she did not scold me. She noticed my shining eyes and sat down to listen to the story of how a hen lays an egg: the wonder of that moment when the egg finally fell to the ground."[49]

Jane's mother had the wisdom to notice and nurture her young daughter's calling. When I first read this account, I was dumbstruck. What a gift that mother had given to her child. "Have I been doing the same with my children?" I wondered. Until that point, my parenting philosophy had been simple—love my children unconditionally. In that moment, I added a second pillar to my approach to parenting—identify and cultivate the essential calling in my children without exception.

The timing of this insight was fortuitous. My daughter had developed a passion for musical theater. I now began to appreciate this passion for what it was—her calling. There was an inner light that was unmistakable. I now began to notice her "shining eyes" whenever she performed. I was proud and envious to see her discover something so sacred and commit to the fulfillment of this calling. Recognizing this as her unique gift, I realized what I had for some time understood intuitively—that my responsibility as her father was to commit everything I had to honoring and supporting her passion from that point forward. I'm proud to say I have never wavered in this commitment.

As a child, you may not have been fortunate enough to have parents, teachers, or other adults in your life who were able to discern and reflect your calling. I certainly didn't, or at least I didn't appreciate or notice the support if it did in fact exist. Perhaps your calling flashed in your shining eyes from time to time but remained dormant throughout your childhood with no one there to nurture it. As an adult, how do you now discern your calling?

I have met and mentored many young adults who ask some form of the same question: "How do I find my purpose in life?" I usually offer the following paradoxical advice: "The harder you search for your purpose, the less likely you are to discover it." I explain that your calling or purpose is like a seed that requires the right conditions to grow. Finding it is more about letting go and creating the conditions for it to emerge, the most important of which is patience. It is about noticing what is already there. Like the gold underneath the stucco on the Buddha statue, it may take years, sometimes decades, for your calling to reveal itself. The key is to let go, be open, and to keep noticing. The more you let go, the quicker your calling will be revealed. Once it emerges, you will know. It will be unmistakable.

There is a reason this chapter comes last. Discovering your calling is perhaps the most challenging of the ten lines of code you will write. It is the most difficult, in part, because it first requires a rewriting of the program that is concerned with looking good and getting ahead. The part of your program that says you're supposed to do this and not supposed to do that. That says you're supposed to go to college, then perhaps graduate school, get a well-paying job, build a family, work hard, earn enough money, and then (and only maybe then) have enough time and be sufficiently healthy to truly enjoy life. Don't get me wrong; this path may very well produce an extraordinary life. But it is highly unlikely to do so unless it is intentional. Unless it is driven by one who has mastered his code. One who is the author of his life. An extraordinary life will not happen out of a subconscious adherence to a series of default rules that are designed to avoid risk and keep you safe. If you are living out of your program, you will not have the consciousness to see your calling. It is only by moving from program to code that you will have the ego maturity to recognize what it is that you are truly meant to do.

In his marvelous book *The War of Art*, Steven Pressfield references the Jungian transition from ego to self as essential to the creative act. The ego is the part of you that is concerned primarily with your psychological protection and the survival of your identity. It is based in fear. It controls you. It doesn't allow for much choice. The self, on the other hand, is all-encompassing. It includes the ego, as well as the personal and collective unconscious. According to Pressfield, when the seat of consciousness shifts from the ego to the self, the space for creation and evolution—for truly living—opens up.

At once we discern what's really important. Superficial concerns fall away, replaced by a deeper, more profoundly grounded perspective . . .

Here's what I think. I think angels make their home in the Self, while Resistance has its seat in the Ego.

The fight is between the two.

The Self wishes to create, to evolve. The Ego likes things just the way they are.[50]

It took me almost four decades to discover my purpose. My essential calling. That which I love to do, that the world needs, that I can get paid for, and that I'm good at. I knew it immediately. My job then became to cultivate it. To do that, we take the next step on the path.

Step Two: Overcome Resistance and Doubt

Once you have identified your calling, the next step is to commit to it fully. To do so is not easy. You must know that there will be significant counterforces that serve as powerful obstacles to fully committing to your calling—the most significant of which are resistance and doubt. Pressfield makes the case that resistance is the most powerful force standing in the way of the creator and her creation:

Resistance cannot be seen, touched, heard, or smelled. But it can be felt. We experience it as an energy field radiating from a work-in-potential. It's a repelling force. It's negative. Its aim is to shove us away, distract us, prevent us from doing our work . . .

Rule of thumb: The more important a call or

action is to our soul's evolution, the more Resistance we will feel toward pursuing it . . .

Resistance has no strength of its own. Every
ounce of juice it possesses comes from us. We feed
it with power by our fear of it.

Master that fear and we conquer Resistance.[51]

How then do you master your fear of resistance?
The key is awareness. Resistance's power comes from
its invisibility. You often fear that which you cannot see.
With awareness, you can begin to use the force of resistance to serve your calling. Awareness was critical for
me while I wrote this book. Often I would feel the pull
away from the act of sitting down and committing to
writing. Rather than fear this counterforce, I embraced
it. I leaned into it. I began to use its energy much like the
aikido master moves *with* his opponent's energy rather
than against it. I began to see resistance like gravity, an
omnipresent energy that, despite its downward pressure, allowed for infinite possibilities of movement and
action.

Like resistance, doubt has the same potential to
oppose the creator. In the *Bhagavad Gita*, the definitive
Hindu guide to dharma, Krishna's advice to Arjuna is
to avoid vacillation or doubt at all costs. This is a key
lesson of the Gita. This does not mean to suggest that
dharma requires arrogance or supreme self-confidence.
Self-doubt is inevitable, and perhaps essential. Again,
Pressfield sums it up perfectly:

Self-doubt can be an ally. This is because it serves
as an indicator of aspiration. It reflects love, love of
something we dream of doing, and desire, desire to

do it. If you find yourself asking yourself (and your friends), "Am I really a writer? Am I really an artist?" chances are you are.

The counterfeit innovator is wildly self-confident. The real one is scared to death.[52]

In writing this book, I regularly questioned my abilities as a writer. "Is this good enough?" "Will anyone really want to read this?" I saw these questions not as an obstacle to my commitment—in fact, they never got in the way of my writing. Instead, I saw them as natural inquiries of a person who cared about his craft and was committed to doing his very best work. It is only the kind of doubt and vacillation that stand in the way of action that must be avoided if you are to truly fulfill your calling. The natural questioning of your abilities, so long as it doesn't paralyze, should be seen as a welcome and normal by-product of your commitment to your creation.

One other way to neutralize the forces of resistance and doubt is to change how you think about them. Although there may be a tendency to vilify these forces, I prefer to normalize (and neutralize) them by thinking about them systemically. The tendency of any living biological system—human or otherwise—is toward stability or homeostasis. This fundamental principle of systems is predictable and inevitable. It is why growth is so hard. You see it in your difficulty keeping New Year's resolutions, in the staying power of dysfunctional families, and in the challenges of organizational change. When you resist the natural forces of homeostasis, you give them power. When you see them and appreciate them for the natural survival forces that they are, you can find ways to leverage them and convert their energy into growth.

Step Three: Commit to the Path of Mastery

Fully committing to your calling requires that you commit to the path of mastery. While we have talked a lot about mastery, we have not fully defined it yet. There are a number of very acceptable definitions. The one I prefer is the following: mastery is a state whereby the master senses being *used by* that which she is mastering. It is the master being used by, as opposed to the master using, that defines mastery. To understand this phenomenon, imagine that I throw a tennis ball toward you without telling you in advance. Assuming you are a person of at least average physical and athletic ability, you will automatically reach for and grab the ball. You will have the sense of being used by the ball. The act of reaching for the ball and grabbing it in midair will occur to you without conscious thought or effort. This is mastery. It is ongoing and never-ending. Like Zeno's paradox of Achilles and the tortoise, each gain may become incrementally smaller and harder to notice, but you will never finish mastery. You can only hope to be on and stay on its path.

So what is the path of mastery? And how do you stay on it? I believe it requires three things:

1. Practice

2. Focus

3. Surrender

First, mastery requires practice. Despite the popularity of the ten-thousand-hour rule—the notion that mastery requires a minimum of that much practice—it is only a certain type of practice that can result in true mastery (and there is no magic to the ten-thousand-hour mark).

Practice that produces true mastery is known as deliberate practice. First characterized by the psychologist Anders Ericsson, deliberate practice has the following key elements that go beyond the qualitative requirement of several hours of daily practice over a sustained period of time. First, you must be extremely motivated. Second, deliberate practice must be focused very specifically on the next step on the path to mastery—the next learning milestone that is just beyond your immediate reach. Practicing something that you have already mastered, while valuable, is not sufficient. George Leonard, in his book *Mastery,* refers to this as "playing the edge," the paradox of both respecting the fundamentals of the craft and constantly and obsessively pushing the limits and taking risks for the sake of higher performance. Third, deliberate practice must contain feedback loops, preferably with the assistance of an outside coach or expert. Finally, practice must not be considered to be separate from mastery. As Leonard writes, "Practice *is* the path of mastery."[53]

The second requirement of mastery is intense focus and discipline, and the ability to say no to the things that are inconsistent with the thing being mastered. In his book *Essentialism*, author Greg McKeown argues, "Only once you give yourself permission to stop trying to do it all, to stop saying yes to everyone, can you make your highest contribution towards the things that really matter."[54] If it were that simple, why wouldn't we all focus on the things that are most important to us? It turns out that saying no is really hard. In the last chapter, we touched on this briefly. We learned that the thing that most often gets in your way of saying no to something is your survival strategies—the need to please, to be liked, to achieve, to be perfect, to be in control. Not surprisingly, the thing that must be mastered first before we can answer our calling full-out is our ego. And, as with most new, conscious behaviors, having the discipline to say no requires a new set of beliefs. As McKeown suggests, "Essentialists see trade-offs [having to say no] as an inherent part of life, not as an inherently negative part of life. Instead of asking, 'What do I have to give up?' they ask, 'What do I want to go big on?' The cumulative impact of this small change in thinking can be profound."[55]

Third, mastery requires full surrender to the fact that the path to achieving it is never-ending. It is like a mountain with no top. There is no final declaration of success. Practice on the path of mastery *is* mastery. To help you understand this, I'd like to share something again from Stephen Cope. In his book, he tells the story of the Japanese artist Katsushika Hokusai, painter of the famous work *The Great Wave off Kanagawa*. Hokusai shared the following, which perfectly captures the spirit of the full surrender to the never-ending nature of mastery:

"From around the age of six," the artist began, "I had the habit of sketching from life." He continues, "I became an artist, and from fifty on began producing works that won some reputation, but nothing I did before the age of seventy was worthy of attention. At seventy-three, I began to grasp the structures of birds and beasts, insects and fish, and of the way plants grow. If I go on trying, I will surely understand them still better by the time I am eighty-six, so that by ninety I will have penetrated to their essential nature. At one hundred, I may well have a positively divine understanding of them, while at one-hundred and thirty, forty, or more I will have reached the stage where every dot and every stroke I paint will be alive. May Heaven, that grants long life, give me the chance to prove that this is no lie."[56]

Step Four: Let Go of the Outcome

While you must commit to mastering your calling, paradoxically you cannot be attached to the outcome. The principle of nonattachment is shared in many traditions. As Gandhi put it, "Satisfaction lies in the effort, not in the attainment. Full effort is full victory." The striving toward the attainment of some end has the perverse effect of pulling you out of the present and away from your calling. To help you understand, let me offer you the distinction between intention and attachment. It is important to have a clear and strong intention, even to an outcome, but to let go of any attachment to that outcome.

I practiced the distinction while writing this book. I committed to not being attached to the outcome of my writing. I *intended* to write a great book that would have a huge impact on a large number of readers. But I renounced any *attachment* to the outcome. If you are reading these words and they are having their intended impact, it will be because I let go of my attachment to any particular outcome and instead allowed the energy of my calling to guide me.

It is wise to heed the words of Thomas Merton, one of the most influential Catholic writers of the twentieth century:

> We cannot achieve greatness unless we lose all interest in being great. For our own idea of greatness is illusory, and if we pay too much attention to it we will be lured out of the peace and stability of the being God gave us, and seek to live in a myth we

have created for ourselves. It is, therefore, a very great thing to be little, which is to say: to be ourselves. And when we are truly ourselves we lose most of the futile self-consciousness that keeps us constantly comparing ourselves with others in order to see how big we are.[57]

Step Five: Have Faith

Letting go of the outcome requires that you have faith in your calling and in your ability to be its servant. In the *Bhagavad Gita*, Krishna tells Arjuna that he does not own or control his dharma, but rather that he must be of complete service to it. This is a fundamental teaching in that, as we become more conscious, we begin to see the connectedness of everything, including ourselves. If you are indeed part of everything, then you can begin to see yourself as an empty vessel into which consciousness flows. In the *Tao Te Ching*, Lao Tzu counsels, "See the world as yourself. Have faith in the way things are. Love the world as yourself; then you can care for all things." We are here to be used by our calling, not to use it. This is the essence of seeing yourself as the vessel for your gift to manifest. Cope describes how the master Beethoven recognized this in himself:

> The music, Beethoven says, seems to be writing itself. The Master now experienced a new dimension of trust in The Gift. He understood that his gift was not personal. That he was not the Doer. That his responsibility was not to create The Gift—that was a done deal—but only to sustain it, to husband it, to nurture it in every way possible.[58]

Pressfield takes a slightly different approach to this notion:

It's as though the Fifth Symphony existed already in that higher sphere, before Beethoven sat down and played dah-dah-dah-DUM. The catch was this: The work existed only as potential—without a body, so to speak. It wasn't music yet. You couldn't play it. You couldn't hear it.

It needed someone. It needed a corporeal being, a human, an artist (or more precisely a genius, in the Latin sense of "soul" or "animating spirit") to bring it into being on this material plane.[59]

The point of this final lesson is not to necessarily take it literally. You do not need to be convinced that you are but a vessel through which the gods bring forth a creation that already exists. Yet having some faith that you are being used to bring forth something you can uniquely create is tantalizing. It will allow you to detach more easily from the outcome and to surrender to your calling.

Step Six: Embrace Your Mortality

It may be surprising to end a chapter on living life on purpose and a book devoted to mastering life with a section on death. Or perhaps, given its perceived finality, death is the perfect subject with which to conclude. Regardless, the fundamental paradox of life and death begs for death's inclusion. As with any paradox, life and death cannot exist without each other. This is an essential teaching of the ancient texts.

But what of death? What purpose does it have in teaching you about life? Almost every ancient tradition speaks to the importance of embracing your impermanence. In the *Tao Te Ching,* it is written that "if you stay in the center and embrace death with your whole heart, you will endure forever." Impermanence is a central tenet of Buddhism, upon which many of its teachings rest. The influential philosopher Martin Heidegger described the anxiety of one's impermanence as "an unshakable joy" because death reminds you that there is no right way to live life. Rather, death is a reminder that you have the responsibility to live your life according to your own choices. For Heidegger, that is the mark of a truly authentic individual.

Of all the philosophies and traditions, perhaps no other group devoted as much attention to the subject of death as the Stoics. In *Letters from a Stoic*, Seneca writes, "You are younger; but what does that matter? There is no fixed count of our years. You do not know where death awaits you; so be ready for it everywhere." The Stoics even advocated a practice of visualizing the death of your loved ones. Upon a first reading, these admonitions to be constantly aware of death may seem morbid or fatalistic. Yet the reminders of death are intended as a wake-up call to live life. With the inevitability of death in the forefront of your mind, the quality of your life will begin to shift. As Marcus Aurelius wrote, "You could leave life right now. Let that determine what you do and say and think."

To remind themselves of death and keep focused on living life on purpose, the Stoics followed an ancient Roman practice called *memento mori*, or reflection on mortality. In Roman times, it was a common practice for a victorious military leader to parade through the adoring masses. The ceremony would last all day, with the general riding in a chariot drawn by four horses. Sitting behind him unnoticed would be a slave whose responsibility was to whisper to him continuously, "Respice post te. Hominem te esse memento. Memento mori!" ("Look behind. Remember thou art mortal. Remember you must die!")

No stranger to the ancient traditions, Steve Jobs practiced a form of *memento mori* and credited much of his creative success to it. In his 2005 commencement speech to the graduating class at Stanford University, Jobs shared the following:

> Remembering that I'll be dead soon is the most important tool I've ever encountered to help me make the big choices in life. Because almost everything—all external expectations, all pride, all fear of embarrassment or failure—these things just fall away in the face of death, leaving only what is truly important. Remembering that you are going to die is the best way I know to avoid the trap of thinking you have something to lose. You are already naked.[60]

Perhaps, then, the discovery of the infinite wisdom inside you must begin with an embrace of death. May this book and the slivers of wisdom within it remind you to begin (or continue) peeling back the layers that mask the glory of who you are.

Epilogue

Everyone longs to be loved. And the greatest thing that we can do is to let people know that they're loved and capable of loving.
—*Fred Rogers*

When I finished writing the final draft of this book, it felt great. I could now finally devote my energies to planning for the book's publication and my mission of having it reach and impact as many people as possible.

Yet there was something still nagging at me. Something that felt missing. In the first draft, I had written a chapter on the importance of being kind. It was a part of the book that felt most vital, and, at the same time, it was the one with which I struggled the most. Kindness is one of those subjects that feels ineffable to me—much easier to experience than to describe in words. Every attempt I made fell short of the impact and originality I desired. So I decided to omit it from the book, satisfying myself that the thread of kindness ran through every chapter, albeit not explicitly.

Then I had an experience that inspired this epilogue, giving me the opportunity to write more directly about kindness and its importance in leading an extraordinary life. It was a normal morning, about a week after I had finished the final draft manuscript. I had taken BART, the Bay Area's subway system, from where I live to the city of San Francisco, where I work. This is my daily commute. Every morning I arrive in the city at the Mont-

gomery Street Station, and I walk about ten minutes up
Montgomery to my office. It has become a very valued
ritual for me. I get to see a wide cross section of the community every morning and every evening on my return
home. Riding the subway allows me to prepare for my
upcoming day and then unwind from and reflect on the
events of the day that has passed. It gives me time to read
and tend to email. I even did some of the writing of this
book on my daily commute.

My walk to and from the Montgomery Street Station
is equally valuable. It gives me a chance to simply soak
in the city or to listen to a podcast or favorite audiobook.
On this particular morning, I was listening to Bruce
Springsteen narrate his extraordinary autobiography,
Born to Run. Every time I walk to and from my office, I
pass people who live on the streets. Our culture refers to
them as "homeless." I prefer to see them just like I see
anyone else, and to see the city as their home. This morning, as I approached the intersection at Montgomery and
Sutter Streets, I noticed a woman sitting on the opposite
corner with her dog and a sign asking for help. This is
a common feature in San Francisco. So normal that the
people who call the city their home blend into the urban
landscape like the buildings, the commuters, and the cars
that fill the streets.

This particular lady stood out to me. She was holding
what appeared to be a cracked, dirty pocket mirror, which
she was angling in front of her face while she meticu-
lously applied mascara to her eyelashes. As I walked by
her, I just knew I had to turn back. It was not conscious.
Rather, it was as if an energy pulled me toward her. I
remember pausing the audiobook I was listening to,
reaching into my wallet, grabbing a five-dollar bill, and
approaching her. She noticed me and slowly put down

the mirror and makeup. I squatted down and extended my hand. And then the following words flowed out of my mouth: "You are already beautiful."

Our eyes locked for about ten seconds, each of us seeing the humanity in the other. She began to smile and radiate, as did I. We each breathed deeply, taking in the beauty of the moment and of each other. I then turned and resumed my trip. The walk that day was like no other I have ever had. It was as if I were floating an inch off the ground. My entire emotional and energetic state shifted. My heart was fully open. I realized in that moment that it was a simple act of kindness that was responsible for transforming the world for me.

Of course, this makes sense. Without kindness, it is impossible to forgive. Without compassion, it is difficult to truly understand. Without loving yourself, it is highly unlikely you will have the courage and discipline to master your own code. Just as all living depends on oxygen, living an extraordinary life requires kindness. Nothing great ever happens without it.

Acknowledgments

We are . . . the sum total of our experiences. Those experiences—be they positive or negative—make us the person we are, at any given point in our lives. And, like a flowing river, those same experiences, and those yet to come, continue to influence and reshape the person we are, and the person we become. None of us are the same as we were yesterday, nor will be tomorrow.
—B. J. Neblett

There is perhaps no more challenging task for an author than to properly acknowledge and appreciate the people who have shaped him. This is certainly my experience. I risk unintentionally leaving out certain individuals who have had a deep impact on me. My hope is that those who have touched my life will know they have done so, and know that I am deeply indebted to them regardless of whether their names are included in the pages of this book.

I must start with my father. As you have seen, he had a profound influence on my beliefs and values. I am forever grateful for his unconditional love and devotion. It is a significant understatement to say that I would not be the man I am today without him.

My wife, Devon, and my children, Jack, Jordan, and Dylan, have been a constant source of inspiration. They bring me joy each day. Much of my strength and passion derives from knowing that I am supported and loved by my immediate family. It was my son Jack's graduation from high school that initially inspired the writing of this book.

I am equally blessed to have an incredible core group of friends. To be seen and understood without judgment is perhaps the most exquisite gift someone can give another human being. They give that to me unfailingly. Thank you.

The wisdom contained in this book comes primarily from three sources. The first are the many great minds throughout history who have taken on the big question of what it means to be human. The work of these philosophers, scientists, leaders, and sages—my teachers, as I think of them—is present throughout this book. They include the ancient masters such as the Buddha, Lao Tzu, Aristotle, and Marcus Aurelius. They are the great philosophers of the last few centuries like Søren Kierkegaard and Martin Heidegger, and the leading psychologists of the twentieth century like Sigmund Freud, Carl Gustav Jung, and Alfred Adler. And finally, there are the modern-day spiritual and personal development teachers such as Byron Katie, Werner Erhard, and Anthony Robbins, who continue to devote their lives to understanding the human condition. I continue to try to devour every word of their teachings.

The second are my amazing partners and colleagues at the Trium Group. I am privileged to work with a team of practitioners who are committed to the mission of changing the world by changing the way business leaders think. In particular, I want to thank Andrew Blum, Catherine Gray, and Jonathan Rosenfeld, who have greatly contributed to my professional growth and self-mastery.

The third are my clients. I am fortunate to work closely with the senior leaders of an incredible group of companies. Many of them are dedicated to making the world a better place. While my role is in some ways that of a teacher, I expect I have learned at least as much from them as I hope they have learned from me.

I am also grateful to have a group of friends, family, and colleagues who read the early drafts of the manuscript and offered honest feedback, much if not all of which contributed to the final version of the book. They include Devon Gold, Jayne Pritchett, Henry Kamali, Gene Frantz, Jonas Leddington, Dugal Bain, Mark Teitell, Will Harper, Gary Storm, Heidi Zak, Christina Stembel, Ben Goorin, Amy Buckner Chowdhry, C. J. Rendic, Carolyn Betts, Seth Cohen, Fred Aslan, Brian O'Keefe, and Kristen Frantz. Each of you made the book immeasurably better.

As any author knows, getting a book published takes a team of dedicated people. I would like to thank the following individuals at Trium—Sarah Holliman, Shannon O'Brien, and Karen Welsh—for their support in the marketing of the book. I was incredibly fortunate to work with the amazing editor Amy Ryan. Credit for much of the book's accuracy and tightness belongs to her. Finally, I owe a huge debt of gratitude to my publisher and trusted guide on this journey, Ben Allen, my production manager, Jade Maniscalco, and their team at Tonic Books. Their mission of creating books that change lives and change the world has been a perfect fit.

Notes

Chapter One

1   http://bulletin-archive.kenyon.edu/x4280.html

2   Robert Kegan, *In Over Our Heads* (Cambridge, MA: Harvard University Press, 1994), 32.

3   This is an important disclaimer. Many popular writers have consciously or unintentionally perpetuated an outdated organizational model of the brain developed in the 1960s by neuroscientist Paul MacLean. His "triune brain" model had three evolutionarily sequential layers. The first is the most ancient, reptilian part at the stem of the brain, which is responsible for automatic or instinctual behaviors and actions and is commonly referred to as the "lizard" part of the brain. The second part is the paleomammalian or "squirrel" region, containing the limbic system, where it is simplistically claimed that the fight/flight/freeze response is located. The final, most evolutionarily recent is the neomammalian or "monkey" part of the brain, where the prefrontal cortex is found. The virtue of this model, and perhaps the main reason for its persistence, is its simplicity. The metaphor allows laypeople and even scientists to make sense of a great deal of complexity. At the same time, modern research has revealed significant flaws and drawbacks to this reductionist representation. With full awareness of its limitations, I have consciously chosen to leverage the simplicity of the model in service to the reader, who is most likely new to the field of neuroscience. Nevertheless, I feel compelled to caution the reader to be aware of the risks of perpetuating a model that often misstates the science. Like many choices, there are trade-offs. I have tried my best to refrain from language that egregiously misrepresents the current state of research. At the same time, I have chosen to oversimplify to avoid the risk of confusion that can come from being too scientifically precise. Finally, I must acknowledge that any description of the structure and workings of the brain and nervous system is likely to be incomplete or obsolete even a decade from now, as the pace of scientific discovery continues to accelerate.

4   For those interested in exploring the research on the brain/ body connection, I recommend Amy Cuddy's book *Presence* (New York: Little, Brown and Company, 2015).

5   Stephen W. Porges, *The Polyvagal Theory: Neurophysiological Foundations of Emotions, Attachment, Communication, and Self-Regulation* (New York: W. W. Norton, 2011).

6   Helen Keller, *Light in My Darkness* (West Chester, PA: Swedenborg Foundation, 2000), 5–6.

7   Ibid.

Chapter Two
8   Lisa Feldman Barrett, *How Emotions Are Made* (Boston: Houghton Mifflin Harcourt, 2017), 40.

9   Ibid., 83.

10   I owe a huge debt of gratitude to the work of Byron Katie. For more information on her work and the process of inquiry, I recommend reading (or listening to) her phenomenal book *Loving What Is* (New York: Harmony Books, 2002).

Chapter Three
11   Robert J. Anderson and William A. Adams, *Mastering Leadership* (Hoboken, NJ: John Wiley & Sons, 2016).

12   https://www.cdc.gov/violenceprevention/ childabuseandneglect/acestudy/ace-brfss.html.

13   Robert M. Sapolsky, *Behave: The Biology of Humans at Our Worst and Best* (New York: Penguin Books, 2017).

14   For a deeper exploration of the relationship between trauma and addiction, I recommend reading Gabor Maté's book *In the Realm of Hungry Ghosts* (Berkeley, CA: North Atlantic Books, 2008).

15   Ibid., 145.

Chapter Four

16   You can take a locus of control test at https://www.darrenjgold.
com/resources.

17   Stephen Nowicki, *Choice or Chance: Understanding Your Locus of Control and Why It Matters* (Amherst, NY: Prometheus Books, 2016).

18   Ibid., 101.

19   Ibid., 118.

20   Shefali Tsabary, *The Conscious Parent* (Vancouver: Namaste Publishing, 2010), 10.

21   Ibid., 13.

22   Peter Drucker, *The Effective Executive* (New York: HarperCollins, 2017), xv.

Chapter Five

23   The work of this program is brilliantly conveyed in the award-winning documentary *The Work*, dir. Jairus McLeary and Gethin Aldous, Blanket Fort Media, 2017.

Chapter Six

24   Thomas Merton, *The Way of Chuang Tzu* (Boston: Shambhala, 2004), 54.

25   Marshall Rosenberg, *Nonviolent Communication* (Encinitas, CA: PuddleDancer Press, 2015), 95.

26   Ibid., 100.

27   See David Bohm, *On Dialogue* (Abingdon, UK: Routledge, 2004).

28   Ibid., 23.

29   Ibid., 14.

30   Ursula K. Le Guin, *Telling Is Listening* (Boston: Shambhala, 2004), 198.

31 Ibid., 196.

32 I have been heavily influenced by the work of Barry Johnson. For an overview, see *Polarity Management: Identifying and Managing Unsolvable Problems* (Amherst, MA: HRD Press, 2014).

33 You can find a polarity map template at https://www. darrenjgold.com/resources.

Chapter Seven

34 https://www.libraryofsocialscience.com/newsletter/ posts/2016/2016-05-12-Galileo.html.

35 Thomas Kuhn, *The Structure of Scientific Revolutions*, fiftieth ann. ed. (Chicago: University of Chicago Press, 2012), 111.

36 Ibid., 76.

Chapter Eight

37 https://www.theguardian.com/books/2015/nov/10/on-the-origin-of-species-voted-most-influential-academic-book-charles-darwin.

38 https://www.omaha.com/money/investors-earn-handsome-paychecks-by-handling-buffett-s-business/article_bb1fc40f-e6f9-549d-be2f-be1ef4c0da03.html.

39 https://time.com/4786837/bill-gates-books-reading/.

40 Alvin Toffler, *Future Shock* (New York: Bantam Books, 1971), 41.

41 Sendhil Mullainathan and Eldar Shafir, *Scarcity* (New York: Times Books, 2013), 60.

42 Carol Dweck, *Mindset*, updated ed. (New York: Ballantine Books, 2016), 6.

43 You can take a growth mindset assessment at https://www. darrenjgold.com/resources.

Chapter Nine

44   See Werner Erhard, Michael C. Jensen, and Steve Zaffron, Integrity: *A Positive Model That Incorporates the Normative Phenomena of Morality, Ethics and Legality*, Harvard Business School NOM Working Paper No. 06-11, September 8, 2006, https://papers.ssrn.com/sol3/papers.cfm?abstract_id=920625.

45   Robert Kegan and Lisa Lahey, "The Real Reason People Won't Change," *Harvard Business Review*, November 2001, https://hbr.org/2001/11/the-real-reason-people-wont-change.

46   You can find an immunity to change template at https://www.darrenjgold.com/resources.

Chapter Ten

47   Stephen Cope, *The Great Work of Your Life* (New York: Bantam Books, 2015), 21–22.

48   Jean Houston, *A Mythic Life* (San Francisco: Harper Collins, 1996), 142.

49   Jane Goodall, "The Story of How a Hen Lays an Egg," Jane Goodall's Good for All News website, May 4, 2016, https://news.janegoodall.org/2016/05/04/story-hen-lays-egg/.

50   Steven Pressfield, *The War of Art* (New York: Black Irish Entertainment, 2002), 136.

51   Ibid., 16.

52   Ibid., 39.

53   George Leonard, *Mastery* (New York: Plume, 1992), 79.

54   Greg McKeown, *Essentialism* (New York: Crown Business, 2014), 4.

55   Ibid., 56.

56   Cope, *The Great Work of Your Life*, 67–68.

57   Thomas Merton, *No Man Is an Island* (Boston: Shambhala, 2005), 128.

58   Cope, *The Great Work of Your Life*, 193.

59   Pressfield, *The War of Art*, 117.

60   "'You've got to find what you love,' Jobs says," News, Stanford University website, June 14, 2005, https://news.stanford. edu/2005/06/14/jobs-061505/.

Made in the USA
Las Vegas, NV
18 August 2021